WONDROUS WOMEN of WALES

Elsie Lily Bentley-Pingree ★ Einir Jones ★ Meleri Jones ★ Seren India Maloney-Jones
Aileen Jackson ★ Mary Jackson ★ Kelly Matulla ★ Ann Matulla ★ Leisa Lloyd Matulla
Ceri Ellis-Jackson ★ Miriam Davies ★ Beatrice Jackson ★ Margaret Jane Jones
Bessie Williams ★ Carys Lili Campbell ★ Meredyth Pabi Campbell ★ Annabella Esme Roberts
Elaine Jones ★ Linda Jones ★ Celyn Mair ★ Seren Ana ★ Millie Pryce ★ Rosie Hawker
Nanw Hywel Edwards ★ Martha Lois Rhys ★ Greta Myfi Rhys ★ Millie Rose Pickup
Efa Martha Jones ★ Cadi Ann Jones ★ Betsan Magi Jones ★ Elinor Makanga
Einir Wyn Hughes ★ Mia Elizabeth Hardy ★ Freja Tallulah Hardy ★ Lily Mai Green
Elsa Megan Green ★ Alys Gwenllian England ★ Hanna Mai England ★ Heledd Anwen Rees
Emilia Minnie Edwards ★ Verity Ruth Carruthers ★ Ffion May Hindmarch ★ Ffion Cait Mills
Nina May Fisher ★ Tia Taylor ★ Rosa Swann ★ Ava Swann ★ Georgia Rogers
Lowri Salisbury ★ Ola Parszewska ★ Noelle O'Hara ★ Sophia Meakin ★ Darcy Johns
Victoria Hughes ★ Florence Gresty-Jones ★ Maisie Garner ★ Ella Cattermole ★ Ezara Brown
Marged Angharad Evans ★ Sofia Arwen Mitchell ★ Eira Hagos Lake ★ Ella Howlett
Ana Heulwen Robles ★ Noelle Emmeline Cook ★ Belle Arthur ★ Isabelle Louise Kelleher
Sofia Barnett ★ Anya Barnett ★ Sofia Roque-Nunes ★ Annabelle Bran ★ Erin Bran
Llio Gethin ★ Mabli Gethin ★ Elan Lois Ifans ★ Popi Mai Evans ★ Ffion Elizabeth Clayton Pugh
Lisa Adcock Williams ★ Lowri Caitlin Thomas ★ Rosabella Smiriglia ★ Lexie Helen Rees
Seren Alexander ★ Fflur Alexander ★ Hazel Leigh ★ Scarlett Rayne ★ Ffion Haf Thomas
Heledd Bizby ★ Ffion Bizby ★ Kitty Elisabeth Grace Davies ★ Megan Elwy John
Branwen Mai Ann Roberts ★ Elinor Gwenith Jenkins ★ Leusa Myfanwy Jenkins
Lowri Menna Jenkins ★ Lily May Lorelei Griffiths ★ Elli Hâf Rees ★ Tirion Mair Rees
Efa Nel Owens ★ Megan Ruth Davies ★ Isobelle Watkiss ★ Liwsi Efa Benson
Sophie Gwynne Benson ★ Harriet Grace Shelley ★ Arianwen Lily Regan
Alana May Lacey-Hastings ★ Anwen Mai Roberts ★ Gwen Elin Roberts ★ Cadi Lois Roberts
Casi Glyn Roberts ★ Peyton Aoibhe Thomas ★ Efa Cadi Morris ★ Awen Haf Morris
Holl Ferched Ysgol Hamadryad ★ Lowri Haf Williams ★ Serenity Jane Mills ★ Ivy Aeryn Mills
Maddison Scarlet Rose Robbins ★ Evie Rose Ord ★ Carys Louise Owens ★ Ede Elizabeth Lewsey
Lois McCarthy ★ Isobel Barnes ★ Sofia Bow ★ Eva Lewis ★ Emilie Halloway

Leusa Miriam Gruffudd ★ Gwenllian Haf Bevan ★ Myfi Huw Bevan ★ Ceinwen France
Seren Phillips ★ Lara Bennett ★ Taleya Thomas-Jones ★ Scarlett James
Eve James ★ Romanni Worrell ★ Tianna Pulman ★ Thea Beatrix Flames ★ Annie MacDonald
Lilly-May Jones ★ Bethan Ritchie ★ Arwen William ★ Lydia May Davies Sexton
Beulah Rose Joan Davies ★ Arianna Minney ★ Carys Burns ★ Charlie Cross ★ Ellie Pearce
Seren Collier ★ Darcy Gwendoline Hope Wolfe ★ Clementine Florence Toni Todd
Ellie Bess Hanson ★ Connie Jane Hanson ★ Rhiannon Elizabeth Starr ★ Mollie Allen
Llinos Eluned Coan Jones ★ Isabelle Williams ★ Evelyn Kate Jane Howard ★ Penelope Hamilton
Nina Figueredo ★ Lois Ruth James ★ Gwen Enid Evans ★ Lyla Grace Jenkins
Lauren Mae Rees Heaton ★ Ella Mae Sadler ★ Evie Scaccia ★ Grace Wade
Josephine Yolanda Elsie Cummins ★ Eleri Mair Hopper ★ Ana Ffion Gregory ★ Sara Elen Gregory
Lara Rebecca Owen ★ Tirion Wyn Davies ★ Jessica Violet Patience Carter ★ Lucy Owen
Lauren Owen ★ Mali Violet Finch ★ Ffion Lilli Woosnam ★ Efa Elizabeth Woosnam
Quinn Elise Michael ★ Carys Anne Whitmore ★ Carys-Haf Tovey ★ Elinor Grieve
Yonna Myfi Edwards ★ Mali Carys Roberts-Lloyd ★ Ffion Celyn Roberts-Lloyd
Yollie Isabella Nicholls ★ Susannah Hope Dobson ★ Eleanor Phelps ★ Megan Grug Fretwell
Elsie Mabel Morris ★ Matilda Mae Morris ★ Pollyanna Hope Morris ★ Cari Enfys Norton
Ffion Williams ★ Aneira Williams ★ Eleri Grace Taylor ★ Carys Olivia Brooks
Jade Jayne Beccano ★ Carys Grace Jones ★ Yvonna Cramer ★ Ffion Chung ★ Miley Chung
Grace Lily Price ★ Emily Bouadana ★ Mari Seddon ★ Nansi Seddon ★ Lily-Rose Price
Bluebelle Marina Price ★ Aurora Grace Hughes ★ Efa Aneira Norris ★ Alaw Emrallt Norris
Florence Adeline Smith ★ Phoebe Nadin Nimmo ★ Michelle Stillwagon ★ Megan Joy Rose
Seren Miller ★ Joanna Miller ★ Isla Miller ★ Eryn Davies ★ Betsan Griffiths
Elena Griffiths ★ Lleucu Wyn Evans ★ Abby Elizabeth Braddon ★ Liza Catherine Braddon
Erica Burtenshaw-Jones ★ Liaba Abbas ★ Nadifo Abdillah ★ Bayan Abdulla ★ Reem Abdulla
Arifa Abedin ★ Isha Adnan ★ Anisha Ahktar ★ Aliyah Ahmed ★ Misbah Ahmed ★ Shadyar Ahmed
Sonia Ahmed ★ Tamanna Ahmed ★ Zainab Ahmed ★ Zaynab Ahmed ★ Zeena Ahmed
Amira Akram ★ Aleeha Ali ★ Amirah Ali ★ Anum Ali ★ Emaan Ali ★ Gusoon Ali ★ Hadiyya Ali
Hassnaat Ali ★ Iram Ali ★ Jamaya Ali ★ Kainaat Ali ★ Maesha Ali ★ Marwa Ali

Mehak Ali ★ Minahil Ali ★ Nayah Ali ★ Nayla Ali ★ Niyla Ali ★ Rhia Ali ★ Sakeena Ali
Samiyah Ali ★ Sumayha Ali ★ Sumayyah Ali ★ Wahba Ali ★ Wajihah Ali ★ Zakirah Alizada
Alesha Amin ★ Mayisha Amin ★ Ramiza Amin ★ Gabriela Anghel ★ Aymelek Avci
Taslima Aziz ★ Anne Marie Babarasul ★ Suraiya Bably ★ Tanisha Bashir ★ Mehreen Batool
Vaiza Batool ★ Wajiha Batool ★ Jumara Begum ★ Maisha Begum ★ Mehak Begum
Murshidah Begum ★ Nadira Begum ★ Taiyabah Begum ★ Tasnia Begum ★ Georgina Branch
Brearna Brown ★ Nela Cervenakova ★ Alexis Cuthbert ★ Shayla Cuthbert ★ Katrina Dunkova
Zuzana Dunkova ★ Selina Faiz ★ Atiya Fatima ★ Olivia Glasgow ★ Aalaa Haji
Michaela Hankova ★ Sawdah Hannan ★ Bethany Holwell ★ Faizah Hussain ★ Fiza Hussain
Maqadas Hussain ★ Sakinah Hussain ★ Sanjida Hussain ★ Zaara Hussain ★ Layla Hussein
Pahmida Islam ★ Senteia Islam ★ Sumaiya Islam ★ Sabrina Jabbar ★ Habiba Jalil
Jennah Kaid ★ Latifa Kaid ★ Dana Kandracova ★ Jana Kandracova ★ Kvetka Kandracova
Magdalena Kandracova ★ Maria Kandracova ★ Sara Kandracova ★ Vanesa V Kandracova
Vanesa Kandracova ★ Samiya Khan ★ Fahmida Khanom ★ Halima Khanom ★ Khahera Khanom
Sarina Khanon ★ Habibah Khatun ★ Sara Kocher ★ Hibah Maclachlan ★ Tahiyah Maliha
Tahseen Malik ★ Areesha Maqbool ★ Daliya Masood ★ Giada Mensah ★ Jasmine Mensah
Mabiya Miah ★ Ikra Mohamed ★ Ilhan Mohamed ★ Itidal Mohamed ★ Malak Mohamed
Aleena Mohammed ★ Yasmin Monteiro ★ Annais Morgan ★ Gabriella Morgan ★ Hazera Mottakin
Taslima Murseda ★ Shahnaaj Naemma ★ Salima Najy ★ Anjuma Natasha ★ Tanisha Natasha
Eliska Navratilova ★ Rhia Nawaz ★ Rupsha Nessa ★ Misbah Noreen ★ Warjin Nuri
Fariha Onima ★ Francesca Pantazi ★ Ecaterina Papp ★ Viera Piskorova ★ Keeley Price
Piper Prowse ★ Humaira Rabiyah ★ Sairah Rahman ★ Samiyah Rahman ★ Tazmin Rahman
Sneha Ravi ★ Fayar Salmon ★ Shanyra Seivwright ★ Manel Shamiri ★ Amina Sheikh
Amira Sheikh ★ Asia Sheikh ★ Jarin Subah ★ Katarina Tatarova ★ Maria Tulejova
Paulina Tulejova ★ Petra Tulejova ★ Mariam Ullah ★ Ruksaar Yeasmin ★ Mun Na Yu
Maryam Zain ★ Masooma Zara ★ Margita Zigova ★ Rachel Zigova ★ Hayden Rose Allman
Tanwen Mari Davies ★ Annest Ceridwen Davies ★ Eirlys Lleucu Davies ★ Isabelle Sophia Parker
Violet Pearl Parker ★ Eva Lili Mary Hall ★ Greta Lili Jones ★ Persephone May Morgan
Ffion Isla Bowden ★ Willow Rose Mahoney ★ Elena Llio Bowyer ★ Efa Amphlett-Jones

Alys Amphlett-Jones ★ Scarlett Plant ★ Poppy Plant ★ Willow Plant ★ Bethan Jo Malpas
Violet James ★ Olivia Williams ★ Lilly-Mai Doran ★ Nia Catrin Harding ★ Tamsin James
Erin Abigail Starkie ★ Josie Anwen Hexter ★ Elsie Mai Haf Westmore ★ Elian Grug Williams
Eila Lowri Beynon ★ Annest Efa Beynon ★ Emilia Louise Henwood ★ Alice Barker
Isabelle Barker ★ Meg Fitzmaurice ★ Gwen Fitzmaurice ★ Megan Elsie Rose Marshall
Rosie May Todd ★ Dilys Medi Doli Lewis ★ Mali Kate ap Ian Evans ★ Betsan Annie ap Ian Evans
Megahn Eleri Cording ★ Seren Ellen Williams ★ Francesca Rose Walsh ★ Eva Murray
Edie Murray ★ Cali Isabel Kent ★ Amelia Iris Doe ★ Olivia Mae Dewhurst
Sioned Hâf Ffion Herco-Thomas ★ Mai Rhianydd Pearce ★ Edie Oliver-Thomas
Eleri Bilbao-Jenkins ★ Megan Bernadette Mullett ★ Gwenllian Sophia James
Imogen Rose Sullivan ★ Madison Grace Thomas ★ Matilda Rose Payne
Elinor Elisabeth Thomas-Lees ★ Megan Elizabeth Watkins ★ Georgie Charlotte Watkins
Magwen Ariadne Roach ★ Lili Marie Jones ★ May Angharad Davies ★ Willow Belle Foster
Harper Elise Foster ★ Heti Glyn Edwards ★ Elsie-Joy Williams ★ Robyn Elizabeth Thomas
Gursharan Kaur ★ Dilpreet Kaur ★ Freya Hughes ★ Martha Charlotte Booth
Faith Olivia Raymond ★ Elin Grug Jones ★ Eira Fflur Jones ★ Lillian Summer Stone
Meredith Robson ★ Cerys Robson ★ Lily Bethan Smith ★ Esther Northwood ★ Sophie Clare Batten
Hannah Megan Read ★ Lauren Carys Read ★ Ruby Scarlett Mary Fish ★ Sofia Brifcani-Parr
Bonnie Haf Collyer ★ Poppy Cari Williams ★ Mia Cadi Pendse ★ Maisie Heledd Jones
Ffion Stone ★ Mollie Bluett ★ Grug Owen Thomas ★ Sara Elizabeth Tudor Williams
Isabella Grace Ellis ★ Amelia Poppy Ellis ★ Lily Rowan Glenc ★ Ruby Edmunds
Erin Taylor ★ Amélie Thomas Folks ★ Darcie Edmunds ★ Lili Mei Jenkins
Beca Angharad Jenkins ★ Marla Rae McDevitt ★ Cadi Anne McDevitt ★ Betsi Martha Widdicombe
Rhosyn Harvey ★ Elinor Felicity Cross ★ Lal Prydderch Ifan ★ Myfi Prydderch Ifan
Celyn Mai Griffiths ★ Megan Haf Griffiths ★ Bela Gwanwyn Delyth Davies
Ani Elsbeth Linda Davies ★ Megan Fflur Lloyd ★ Mari Elin Lloyd ★ Malen Grug Lloyd
Cadi Mai Glanville ★ Heti Mai Glanville ★ Ruby Clare Sylvia Werrett ★ Eluned Myfanwy Evans
Grace Mae Rees-Jones ★ Megan Rose Rees-Jones ★ Ruby May Evans ★ Nia Megan Jones
Elin Lowri Collins ★ Cariad Rachael Ivy Evans ★ Sara Mair Mifsud ★ Tirion Haf Jones

First impression: 2022
© Medi Jones-Jackson & Y Lolfa Cyf., 2022
Illustrations © Telor Gwyn
Design: Dylunio GraffEG/Dyfan Williams
Cover design: Dylunio GraffEG/Dyfan Williams

This book is subject to copyright and may not be reproduced by any means except for review purposes without the prior written consent of the publishers.

The publishers wish to acknowledge the support of the Books Council of Wales.

ISBN: 978-1-80099-235-1

Published and printed in Wales on paper from well-maintained forests by
Y Lolfa Cyf., Talybont, Ceredigion SY24 5HE
e-mail ylolfa@ylolfa.com
website www.ylolfa.com
tel 01970 832 304

WONDROUS WOMEN OF WALES

Medi Jones-Jackson

Illustrations by Telor Gwyn

y olfa

This book belongs to

------------------------------,

who is wondrous too.

To Anest and Gwenith for your smiles and support.

To Paul and Elis for your love and laughter. YNWA

Medi xxx

LETTER FROM THE AUTHOR

DEAR FRIEND,

In *Wondrous Women of Wales* I've selected women to inspire you. Each one is different, but all of them are connected to Wales — just like you. I hope you'll enjoy learning more about them.

There are stories about overcoming difficulties, stories full of bravery and faith, about winning a race or arriving at the top — 25 stories to motivate and inspire.

Life is meant for living, so make the decision now to have a life filled with adventure, compassion and bravery, just like the women in the pages that follow.

Keep reading.

Be wondrous!

Medi

THE WONDROUS WOMEN

AMY DILLWYN
14

HALEY GOMEZ
20

BETSI CADWALADR
16

JADE JONES
22

KATE BOSSE-GRIFFITHS
18

FRANCIS HOGGAN
24

MAIR RUSSELL JONES 26	 **ANGHARAD TOMOS** 34
EILEEN BEASLEY 28	 **TORI JAMES** 36
BETTY CAMPBELL 30	 **GWENDOLINE & MARGARET DAVIES** 38
LAURA ASHLEY 32	**VULCANA** 40

ANN PETTITT
42

RACHEL ROWLANDS
50

CRANOGWEN
44

MARGARET HAIG THOMAS
52

LOWRI MORGAN
46

ANNIE ATKINS
54

MARY VAUGHAN JONES
48

MARY QUANT
56

SHIRLEY BASSEY 58

MEENA UPADHYAYA 62

LUCY THOMAS 60

GLOSSARY 64
ACTIVITIES 65
TIMELINE 88

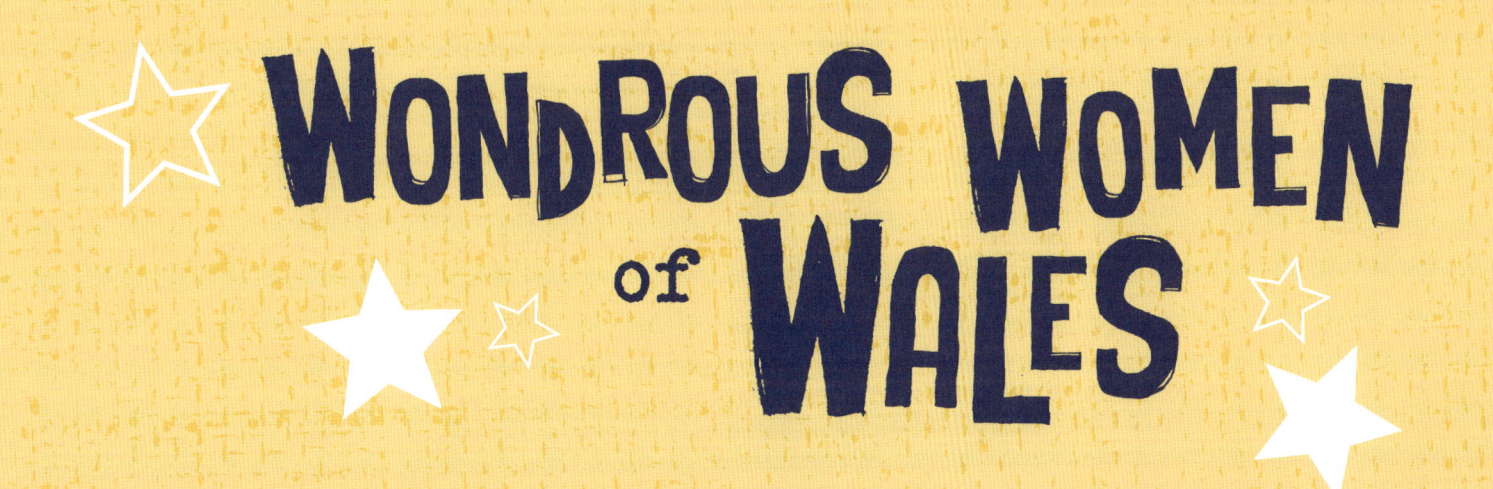

Wondrous Women of Wales

AMY DILLWYN

Sketty, Swansea 1845-1935

Wales' first businesswoman... and a real rebel

Despite growing up in a rich household, Amy Dillwyn always believed in trying to make the world around her a better place for anyone less fortunate than her.

Her family were wealthy industrialists, but her comfortable world was turned upside down when her mother, brother and father all died one after another.

Her father had been a wonderful man but a terrible businessman. Hundreds of people were employed at their zinc factory but when he died, he left the company in severe debt – around £8 million in today's money. Who could get them out of this mess?

AMY TO THE RESCUE!

Saving the factory would involve a lot of sacrifices, including personal ones from Amy. She had to leave the lovely grand house she grew up in. She sold the contents too: the furniture, countless works of art, her grandfather's gold medals – even down to the servants' scrubbing brushes. She moved into a modest little rented house.

Amy saw the potential in the zinc factory. With her constant hard work, determination and perseverance, she paid off all the debts and turned the company's fortunes around. It thrived with her in charge. Hurray! The workers were so grateful to her.

AMY'S AIMS
- Save the company and jobs
- Re-establish her family's good name

"I am becoming a man of business," Amy wrote in a letter to a close friend.

Amy became world famous as a prominent figure in business. Her business brain was second to none, at a time when women in high-powered jobs didn't exist.

For the rest of her life, she used her new-found status to fight for women's rights – always challenging, always fighting: a true rebel heart.

3 facts about zinc
- Chemical element (symbol: Zn)
- A bluish-white metal
- Put on top of iron and steel to stop them rusting

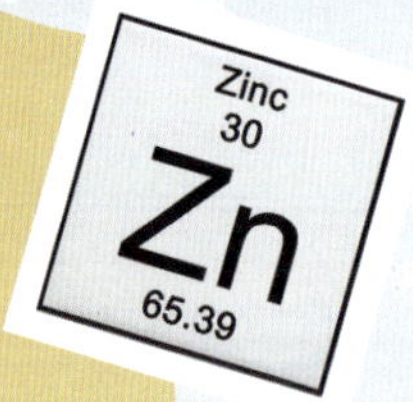

Zinc 30 Zn 65.39

SAY CHEESE!

Amy's big sister Mary was one of the first photographers in Wales and the first person ever to photograph a snowman.

MONTE CARLO

After retiring, Amy's main hobbies were water polo and gambling at casinos in Monte Carlo (not at the same time, I hope!).

Amy loved smoking cigars (very unladylike at the time!).

Newspaper from 1902

PALL MALL GAZETTE

"ONE OF THE MOST REMARKABLE WOMEN IN GREAT BRITAIN"

Reason v. fashion

Amy was a big supporter of the Rational Dress Movement, which aimed to change the way women dressed.

Amy believed that women should dress for comfort.

Fashion of the day

- Whalebone corset pulling tummies in super-tight
- Many, many layers of petticoats topped with a heavy skirt
- High heels
- Bustle to make your bottom more shapely
- Tight cloak – restricting arm movement

= can't move, can hardly breathe, causing long-term injuries

Amy's fashion

- Practical hat
- Tailored jacket and simple blouse
- Unfussy skirt
- Flat boots

= healthy, sensible, and practical

ELIZABETH 'BETSI' CADWALADR

Llanycil, Bala 1789–1860

Nursing the sick

Meet Betsi Cadwaladr. Born into a family of 16 children (yikes!), she didn't find working as a maid in the local hotel in Bala very fulfilling. This was the life a girl like her was expected to have, but Betsi was about to defy expectation.

In the middle of the night, Betsi tied her bed sheets together, climbed out of the window and ran away. What an escape!

First she went to Liverpool, then London, then our adventurous gal found herself on board a ship as a captain's maid. Adventure called, and Betsi answered!

She travelled to the furthest corners of the world – China, India, Australia, and South America. This was at a time where people rarely went 10 miles from where they were born.

Many of the passengers or sailors got ill at sea and Betsi helped nurse them better. She even helped a baby or two into the world. She had found her true calling and returned to Guy's Hospital in London to officially train as a nurse.

Like the rest of Britain, Betsi read in the newspapers about the Crimean War (1853–1856). Britain and France and the Ottoman Empire were at war with Russia. Betsi went out there to help nurse the injured soldiers.

Conditions were terrible. Disease and infections killed more soldiers than the actual fighting. Betsi believed that providing clean conditions for the soldiers would mean fewer men died. She was right.

By now Betsi was 65. Most women during this time only lived to 45. Yet she worked over 20 hours a day, sleeping on the hard floor when she was tired.

TO BE OR NOT TO BE

Betsi loved a good show. She'd even entertain crews on board ships by performing snippets of William Shakespeare's plays.

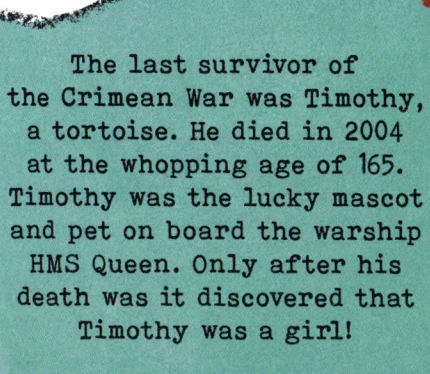

Crimea

Before nurses like Betsi (and also Florence Nightingale and her famous lamp) went to Crimea, ten times more soldiers died of diseases than of battle wounds.

"No!" x 20

In the book about her life, Betsi said 20 men had asked for her hand in marriage.

5 years after the Crimean War

The French scientist Louis Pasteur proved that microscopic organisms called germs caused diseases.

When she returned to Wales, she was exhausted. She'd lived an amazing life and she contacted an author to write her life story — the places she'd been, the things she'd seen, all those adventures.

Today, the Betsi Cadwaladr Health Board in north Wales, named in her honour, employs over 17,000 staff, giving valuable medical care to nearly 700,000 people. Betsi would be so proud.

Before Betsi:
- Sharing dirty beds ✓
- 14 baths for 2,000 soldiers ✓
- Sharing dirty dishes ✓
- Filthy walls and floors ✓
- Terrible food ✓
- Revolting toilets ✓
- No soap ✓
- Lice ✓
- Rats ✓
- More rats ✓

DID YOU KNOW?

165

The last survivor of the Crimean War was Timothy, a tortoise. He died in 2004 at the whopping age of 165. Timothy was the lucky mascot and pet on board the warship HMS Queen. Only after his death was it discovered that Timothy was a girl!

KATE BOSSE-GRIFFITHS

Egyptologist: from Germany to Egypt to Swansea

Wittenberg-am-Elbe, Germany
1910–1998

1933 – the Nazi party were voted into power in Germany. They were bullies and started making life difficult for thousands of people – people they saw as enemies, including Jews. Before long, innocent people were sent to jails and concentration camps. This was such a scary time.

Those who could leave Germany did, leaving behind their homes, families and friends.

Kate Bosse-Griffiths faced this very dilemma – she was no longer allowed to work or study in Germany once the Nazi party discovered that her mother's family were Jewish.

Kate boarded a ship and came to Britain. She was an Egyptologist – specialising in the art and history of ancient Egypt. While in Oxford, she met and fell in love with a young Welshman, J. Gwyn Griffiths.

They married, but her husband wasn't the only thing Kate fell in love with. She fell in love with Wales too.

"I fell in love with the Welsh mountains. It was love at first sight," she wrote to a friend.

They settled in Swansea and Kate worked at the university, which had thousands of priceless artefacts from ancient Egypt in its collections.

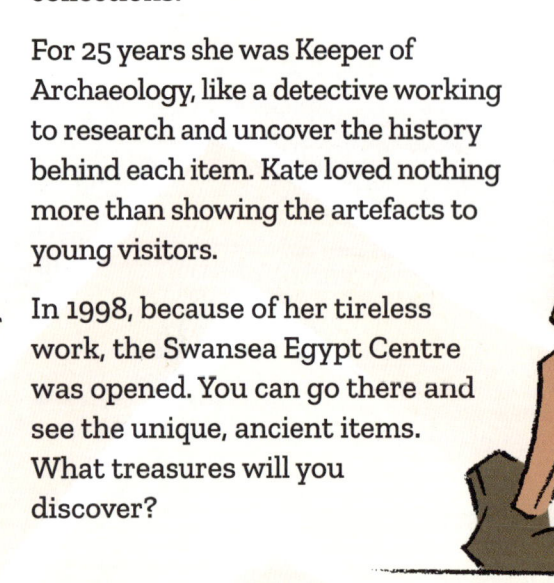

For 25 years she was Keeper of Archaeology, like a detective working to research and uncover the history behind each item. Kate loved nothing more than showing the artefacts to young visitors.

In 1998, because of her tireless work, the Swansea Egypt Centre was opened. You can go there and see the unique, ancient items. What treasures will you discover?

Nazi Germany – a dark chapter in history

World War II (1939–1945) left a horrible scar on history. Towns and cities were bombed and destroyed. Millions of innocent victims died, including over six million Jews, in the Holocaust. Kate never again saw her mother, who was murdered at Ravensbrück concentration camp.

So far, over 130 pyramids have been discovered in Egypt.

WELCOME TO THE MUSEUM

LIFE AFTER DEATH

The Egyptians believed the dead needed their earthly bodies in the afterlife. Bodies were mummified ready for when the afterlife called.

Image: iStockphoto

HALEY GOMEZ

Barry 1979-

Astrophysicist - seeing the whole universe in a speck of stardust

Everything started for Haley when her teacher gave her a book as a gift. Not just any book – a book about space.

The gift was the spark for a lifelong love of space and astrophysics. Haley read the book and another after that, then another after that. She loved all things space. Before long she was studying astrophysics at Cardiff, the first of her family to go to university. Today she is an expert on space and astrophysics. She lectures at the university and visits schools to get kids just like you interested in space and help inspire the next generation of space scientists.

Haley's specialism is cosmic dust – how, where and when it was created.

Haley uses data from satellites and space telescopes like the Herschel Telescope. Because of Haley and scientists like her, we know more about space and the universe than ever, but we still have a long way to go, and scientists are learning new things every single day.

Haley was inspired by Vera Rubin - a pioneering astronomer from America.

Travels with a telescope

Inspired by Haley? Grab your coat and spend time stargazing. Wales has some great spots for spotting a shooting star or two.

- Snowdonia National Park
- Brecon Beacons National Park
- Elan Valley
- Pembrokeshire Coast National Park

Look out for stargazing events in your area.

Well, I never!

Space is really, really old and like other old things, it's very dusty. This dust is so small. It's about 0.1 mm in diameter – roughly the same as the average human hair.

What is astrophysics?

Great question. Astrophysicists study how planets and stars work and how the universe was created.

14,000,000,000

HAPPY BIRTHDAY TO YOU

How old our universe is – that's a lot of candles for one birthday cake!

The Herschel Space Telescope

- Sent into space from the Guiana Space Centre in South America
- Travelled 1,500,000 km through space, sending data back to scientists on Earth
- Was the largest infra-red telescope sent into space
- Interior mirror a whopping 3.5 metres in length

In 2020 Haley Gomez won the Frances Hoggan medal! Congratulations, Haley!

14.5 t

14.5 TONNES

The amount of extra-terrestrial matter (stuff from space) that falls on Earth every day. That's about four elephants' worth of dust.

OUCH!

JADE JONES

Flint's golden girl

'Taekwondo Club – beginners welcome!' read the poster Jade's grandad saw on the leisure centre noticeboard.

"Perfect for Jade," he thought. "This will keep her out of trouble."

At 8 years old, Jade attended her first taekwondo class at Flint Leisure Centre. She came out of class beaming. She loved it.

She continued to attend classes week after week, growing in confidence. Her lovely grandad, Martin, drove her back and forth to Manchester on weekdays and Cardiff at the weekends so Jade could train with the country's best taekwondo coaches.

Flint 1993–

All in the name
Flint's leisure centre is now called the Jade Jones Pavilion.

In Jade they saw both talent and potential. So did the community of her hometown. They raised money to send Jade to the World Championships. She got to the final, where she lost to Hou Youzou of China.

She was disappointed but the Olympic Games in London were just around the corner – it would be her time to shine.

She reached the final and who stood between her and a gold medal? Hou Youzou. They faced each other, bowed, and fought. The final scoreboard showed 6-4. Jade was an Olympic gold medallist.

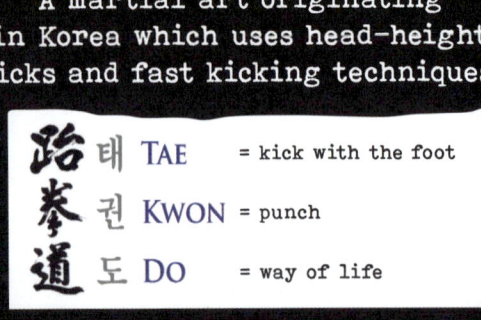

WHAT IS TAEKWONDO?

A martial art originating in Korea which uses head-height kicks and fast kicking techniques.

跆 태 TAE = kick with the foot
拳 권 KWON = punch
道 도 DO = way of life

Taekwondo principles
- courtesy
- honesty
- perseverance
- self-control
- indomitable spirit

JADE'S TRAINING SCHEDULE

9 a.m.–noon gym, running and weight training

2–3 p.m. rest

4–6 p.m. gruelling taekwondo session

EVERY DAY!

She threw her helmet in the air and ran around the ring with the Welsh flag. The crowd went mad.

"It doesn't feel real – it feels crazy. It's the best moment of my life." JJ on winning the 2012 gold medal.

Back in Flint, hundreds of her supporters watched their girl stand proudly on top of the podium, a shiny gold medal around her neck. All her hard work had paid off.

Four years later she added to her medal collection with another gold from the Rio Olympics. Double Olympic champion.

She lost her bid to win a third gold medal in the Tokyo Olympics in 2021, but one of her fans noted, "You have brought glory to Wales and you stand alongside some of the greatest Olympians in history."

Jade is a true inspiration to generations of young girls.

57kg Jade's fighting weight category

A post box in Flint was painted gold to commemorate her 2012 victory.

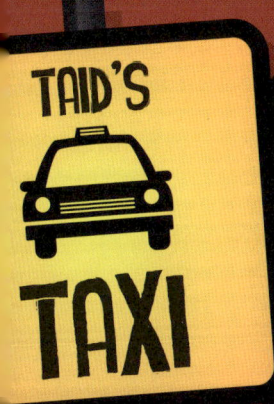

TAID'S TAXI

39,104 MILES Average mileage Martin drove in a year, taking Jade to all her training sessions. A gold medal to Martin too, please!

DON'T TRY THIS AT HOME
Jade's nickname is 'The Headhunter' because she loves scoring points by kicking her opponent's head. Ouch!

Frances Hoggan

Britain's first fully qualified female doctor

Brecon 1843-1927

Women today can succeed in so many different careers. The possibilities are truly endless – astronaut, lorry driver, teacher, film director, deep sea diver, Prime Minister...

But these opportunities weren't always available. There was a time when girls weren't even allowed to go to school. Imagine that!

One who thought this wasn't right was Frances Hoggan from Brecon. She believed that little girls were just as clever as little boys. They deserved to go to school too. Luckily for her, her mam and dad also believed this.

Good, because Frances was very clever and flourished at school. She had one dream – Frances longed to be a doctor.

Again, this is a simple enough dream for girls nowadays – work hard and apply yourself and you could be in with a chance. But Frances was born in the Victorian age, over 179 years ago. Girls didn't become doctors, however hard they studied.

"No!" "No!" "No!" was the answer Frances got from every university.

Yes, Frances was clever, but more importantly, she was determined. Nothing, especially not the fact that she was a girl, would stand in her way.

At last, she found a university that said "Yes!" and off she and her bulging suitcase went to catch the train to Zurich in Switzerland.

In 1870 Frances graduated with a degree in medicine.

She was now a fully qualified doctor – the UK's first female one. She opened a practice specialising in women's and children's illnesses.

She travelled far and wide and spent the rest of her life fighting to ensure girls got the education they deserved, just like she did.

DR & DR

Frances married Dr George Hoggan – they became the first ever pair of married doctors.

A CLEVER, CLEVER GIRL

5 – number of years it took to graduate with a medical degree

3 – number of years Frances took

FRANCES HOGGAN MEDAL

Frances' name lives on in the medal awarded to a Welsh woman who specialises and excels in politics, medicine, engineering, technology or mathematics.

FH

Frances studied in several countries:

- Wales
- Switzerland
- France
- Germany
- Ireland

6,016 THE NUMBER OF FEMALE DOCTORS WORKING IN THE NHS IN WALES NOW

+GREAT!+

संस्कृतम्

Sanskrit

Frances also became fluent in the Indian language Sanskrit while studying for her medical degree.

25

MAIR RUSSELL JONES

Super codebreaker

Pontycymer 1917–2013

Walking down the street in Cardiff, a stranger tapped on Mair Russell Jones' shoulder. "I hear you're good at solving puzzles and speak fluent German?"

He was right. At the start of the Second World War (1939–1945), Mair was studying German and Music at Cardiff University. She loved crosswords and maths puzzles.

The stranger then posed a challenge — to finish a crossword in less than 12 minutes.

Of course, Mair passed the test, and she was whisked off to help with the war effort. Mair found herself in Bletchley Park, which was buzzing with mathematicians and inventors.

The Germans were sending coded messages to each other using a special machine called the Enigma. If the Bletchley Park team could crack the codes and read the messages, it would help win the war.

Bletchley was so top secret, its name was never used — it was simply called Station X.

Why choose Mair?
- Spoke German ✓
- Read music ✓
- Liked puzzles ✓
- Understood maths ✓
- Could keep a secret ✓

Everyone who worked there had to sign the Official Secrets Act. Mair told no one at all about it for over 50 years.

"The four years I spent at Bletchley Park were among my happiest. I [enjoyed] the knowledge that I was part of one of the most exciting teams that ever represented Britain." MRJ

Today Bletchley Park is a museum, highlighting the important work done there by the codebreakers. You can visit and see Hut 6, where Mair cracked codes with the rest of Bletchley's top-secret army.

DID YOU KNOW?

Maths genius Alan Turing also worked at Bletchley. There he created machines that helped crack the Enigma code and laid the foundations for the computers and artificial intelligence we use today!

What was the Enigma Machine?

- German coding machine to send secret messages
- Messages sent encrypted
- The Germans believed no one would ever be able to understand the messages

HOW DID THE ENIGMA MACHINE WORK?

A bit like a computer keyboard – but when you typed a letter, a different letter would automatically be used.

Original message: I LOVE WALES

Coded Enigma message: A CPBO TICON

Mair's job was to look for patterns in the code.

Station X Top secret mission

Given by Prime Minister Winston Churchill: Read, decipher and solve the secret coded enemy messages.
Help win the war.

Bletchley Park in numbers

12000 – number of people working at Station X (8,000 of them women)

1460 – number of days it took to crack the Enigma machine

6000 – number of messages intercepted by Bletchley daily

It's believed that the work of Bletchley Park shortened the war by 2-4 years, saving around 21,000,000 lives.

GOOD JOB, BLETCHLEY. GOOD JOB, MAIR.

Eileen Beasley
Standing up for the Welsh language

Henllan Amgoed 1921-2012

Sometimes big things start out small. Eileen Beasley's story started when a small brown envelope landed on her doormat. It was a letter from Llanelli Council asking them to pay their council tax. In English.

"I can't make sense of this," Eileen said to her husband Trefor. "Everyone round here speaks Welsh, the council workers speak Welsh, so why are the letters in English?"

In that second, the Beasleys came to a decision – until the Welsh language was treated equally to the English language and their bill was in Welsh too, they would not pay. They took a stand.

Even though they had children to feed – they did not pay.

Even though some people judged them harshly – they did not pay.

This continued for long, difficult years. They were taken to court, but they stood their ground. To try to force the Beasleys to pay, the council sent in the bailiffs to intimidate them. Bailiffs go to your house if you don't pay your debts, and take your belongings.

The bailiffs took their piano, sofa, desk, carpet, crockery and wedding gifts. They even took the children's toys. The only thing they didn't take was Trefor's homemade jam!

Dear Eileen...
Eileen received hundreds of letters of support from around the world – from as far away as America.

✗ Beasley

Did you know? There are 7,117 known languages in the world. Welsh has existed for about 1,100 years.

In 1958 Eileen won an election and became one of the first women in Wales to be an elected councillor.

In an almost empty house, the Beasleys still stood their ground.

In 1960 another small brown envelope landed on the Beasleys' doormat. It was a letter from Llanelli Council asking the Beasleys to pay their council tax.

Only this time the letter was bilingual! There was a Welsh letter alongside the English letter.

The Beasleys had won. They paid their bill.

Today, because of Eileen's protest, the Welsh language has official status.

Thanks, Eileen.

Why not pay?

- They spoke Welsh ✓
- Most of the people in the village spoke Welsh ✓
- Their County Council spoke Welsh ✓
- Official status for the Welsh language ✗
- Welsh language signs ✗
- Bilingual forms ✗

Eileen and Trefor were sent to court 16 times – asking every time for the case to be in Welsh.

Image: Freepik

There's a plaque on their house in Llangennech to remember their protest.

29

BETTY CAMPBELL

Inspirational teacher

Tiger Bay, Cardiff 1934-2017

On the bustling streets of the world's busiest shipping docks, Tiger Bay in Cardiff, in a poor but colourful community of over 50 nationalities, a little girl was born.

Life wasn't easy for Betty Campbell. Her dad was killed in the Second World War when she was just 8. Her mam decided to work doubly hard to give Betty a fair shot in life.

Betty just loved to read and won a scholarship to attend secondary school. Hers was one of the few black faces amongst the crowd of students, but Betty just saw herself as one of the girls.

She longed to be a teacher but her school's headteacher cruelly told her one day that no one would give a black girl like her the opportunity to teach. Too many obstacles stood in her way.

"I went back to my desk and cried," remembered Betty, "but it made me more determined. I was going to be a teacher."

And so it was. Betty spied an article in the local paper advertising a new teacher-training college taking on female students.

"I will be one of those students", Betty told her mother.

And she was. She passed her course and went to teach in Llanrumney, before returning to teach in the Cardiff docks.

A FITTING MONUMENT

There is a statue of Betty in Cardiff Central Square. Have you seen it?

> "Betty achieved her dream through hard work and perseverance and broke down barriers for others to follow."
>
> Wales' former First Minister, Carwyn James

In the 1970s, Betty made history as Wales' first ever black headteacher. She had a mission – to instil pride in her pupils for the colour of their skin and where they came from, and to get black history taught in schools.

"I was going to let the children know that there were black people doing great things." BC

Betty began a big project on Nelson Mandela. Mount Stuart Primary School pupils wrote letters to South Africa. In 1998 President Mandela came to Cardiff, and who did he visit? Why, Betty and her school, of course.

At the end of a long career, Betty had done more than just teach. She inspired generations of children from Cardiff docks to take pride in themselves and their home patch too.

> "Betty made us feel like we could achieve anything."
>
> Betty's student Becky, who now teaches at Mount Stuart

WHO WAS NELSON MANDELA?

In South Africa, black people weren't given the same rights as white people. This was called Apartheid. Mandela spent 27 years in prison for protesting this inequality. On his release he was elected South African President, ended Apartheid and won the Nobel Peace Prize. He died in 2013.

Tiger Bay

It's an odd name, isn't it? It comes from the fierce currents in the local tidal stretches of the River Severn around the docklands area. The famous singer Shirley Bassey comes from Tiger Bay too.

LAURA ASHLEY

Dowlais 1925-1985

Fashion and textile designer

Spots, stripes and squares – look around you: patterns are positively everywhere.

One person who loved patterns, especially flowery patterns, was Laura Ashley. Laura would spend hours and hours at the V&A Museum in London looking at the exhibitions of historical dresses.

She left each time feeling inspired, and one day Laura and her husband Bernard made a life-changing decision – they started a fashion business called... Laura Ashley, after Laura of course.

They invested £10 to buy fabric, dyes and a printing press. In their small flat they started printing fabric, including scarves and tea towels, to sell in local markets. And sell they did – people loved them.

Soon they started making dresses and women loved them too. The dresses were long, romantic, flowery and frilly. Everyone wanted to get their hands on a Laura Ashley dress.

All too soon their success meant their flat was just too small, and when a flood destroyed their first factory in Kent, they packed up their belongings and moved to Machynlleth.

> "I like things that last forever."
> — LA —

LONDON, PARIS, LLANIDLOES

THIS BUILDING WAS THE LOCATION OF LAURA ASHLEY'S FIRST SHOP

A plaque sits on the wall of 35 Heol Maengwyn in Machynlleth, noting its importance as the first ever Laura Ashley shop.

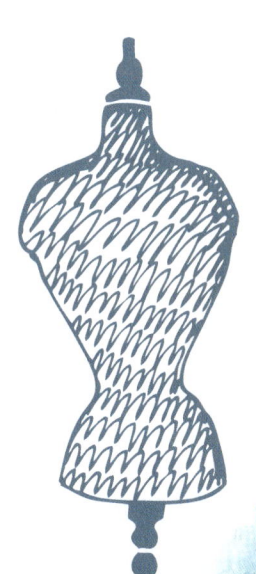

DID YOU KNOW?

Laura was born at her grandma's house in Dowlais because her London-based parents wanted their baby to be born in Wales.

Laura's first shop opened in 1962 at 35 Heol Maengwyn, Machynlleth, with the family cosily living above the shop. Laura designed and used her creative skills and Bernard looked after the business side. They expanded to design things like curtains and wallpaper too. Laura Ashley became a household name.

One day, she and Bernard drove past the old train station in Carno, Powys. This was the perfect place to grow their business and by 1984, sales grossed $130 million internationally. Laura Ashley had a base in Mid Wales for almost 60 years and whilst Laura Ashley shops opened around the world, the plaque above each shop read 'Laura Ashley: London, Paris, Llanidloes'.

There were 500 Laura Ashley shops internationally.

4000
The Fulham Road, London Laura Ashley shop sold a whopping 4,000 dresses in one week.

Geneva, Switzerland
Location of first international Laura Ashley shop

"She changed the look of houses and the way people dressed in an astonishing way. It was the work of a genius."

British VOGUE

Angharad Tomos

Llanwnda 1958–

Opening up a world of imagination

With four sisters, Angharad grew up with a ready-made audience to entertain. Even as a young child, she created miniature storybooks for their dolls.

Those books were the start of an impressive writing career, covering children's and adult books. Angharad's books for grown-ups have won numerous awards at the National Eisteddfod, but for many she's best known as the author of a series of children's books about a mischievous little witch called Rwdlan.

The humble beginnings of the series started when Angharad attended a free art course for unemployed youngsters in the 1980s. She drew a sweet older witch, her pet black cat and her naughty sidekick, Rwdlan. She originally wrote 16 books of adventures for these characters in Welsh, each with artwork from Angharad too.

Nearly 40 years later, the books are as popular as ever. Angharad even created a special version in 2020 when the characters went into lockdown too.

Recently she has published books for young people in English. They often look at events in Welsh history – like *Paint!*, which follows the story of a 12-year-old boy in 1969, the year of the Apollo moon landings and Prince Charles' Investiture in Caernarfon Castle.

Like any great author, Angharad is never scared to take on difficult subjects, including racism and slavery. Her book *Woven* is a moving story set in Penrhyn Castle outside Bangor, about a slave girl taken from her family in Jamaica striking up a friendship with a young Welsh maid. Angharad's aim is to educate young readers about tough chapters of Welsh history.

"No one is ever too young to start making books." AT

Rwdlan

NEW WELSH LANGUAGE ACT!

For decades Angharad has been a prominent member of *Cymdeithas yr Iaith* (The Welsh Language Society), campaigning for the Welsh language.

She went to prison a number of times for protesting and painting a slogan on Nelson's Column in Trafalgar Square. Not one to waste time, Angharad wrote a few books in prison.

Dear Diary...

Angharad keeps a diary, after being inspired by the famous diarist Anne Frank.

"I've been writing all my life." AT

DID YOU KNOW?

Angharad has written a book about Eileen Beasley's protest – it's a small world!

There's a sculpture of Angharad at Glynllifon Park near Caernarfon.

1969 PROTEST

In 1969, Charles became Prince of Wales at Caernarfon Castle. Many in Wales believed that Llywelyn the Last, who was killed by the English army in 1282, was the last true Prince of Wales and that Charles, as an Englishman, should not have the title. This belief led many to protest.

TORI JAMES

Standing on top of the world

Haverfordwest 1981–

Baking with her mam-gu, Tori strained with all her might. The lid of the jam jar simply refused to budge.

"I can't open it!" cried Tori.

"*Twt,*" said Mam-gu. "There's no such word as 'can't'!"

Mam-gu was right. With a final effort, Tori opened the jar and they both enjoyed their homemade Victoria sponge cake with a nice cup of tea.

Tori never forgot the lesson she learnt that day – there's no such word as 'can't': perseverance is key.

Now all grown up, Tori loves nothing more than undertaking adventures in the great outdoors.

1 MOUNTAIN, 4 NAMES

Everest has different names in different countries:

सगरमाथा Sagarmāthā (head of the sky) – Nepal

ཇོ་མོ་གླང་མ Chomolungma (holy mother) – Tibet

珠穆朗玛峰 Zhūmùlǎngmǎ Fēng – China

Everest – named after Welsh surveyor Sir George Everest

EVEREST

- World's highest mountain
- In the Himalayas, between Nepal, Tibet and China
- 4,742 miles west of Wales
- It grows 4 mm a year (40 cm in 100 years)
- Summit 8,848 m (that's 8 Wyddfa/Snowdons on top of each other)

DANGER!

TEMPERATURES -60°C

AVALANCHES

AIR SO THIN YOU CAN HARDLY BREATHE

ICE SHEETS FALLING

200+ MPH WINDS

Essential packing to climb Everest

- Warm hat
- Snowsuit of duck feathers
- Sunglasses – the sun bounces off the snow and blinds you
- Oxygen tanks
- Fleece jacket
- Another coat
- Fleece trousers
- Sturdy boots
- Gloves
- Thermal vest and leggings
- Thick red socks

IMAGINE 643 DOUBLE-DECKER BUSES

ON TOP OF ONE ANOTHER – THAT'S EVEREST'S HEIGHT WOW!

One adventure was calling to her – climbing Mount Everest.

After 18 months' training and three more camping at the foot of the mountain waiting for good weather (bad weather could prove lethal), she was ready.

On 27th May 2007, Tori put on her specialist equipment (including her favourite red socks). After ten hours of non-stop climbing, she reached the summit. For a moment, the highest point on earth had a Welsh girl on top of it, waving the Welsh flag.

She did it! Tori became the first (and as yet only) Welsh woman to conquer Mount Everest.

"If a girl from Pembrokeshire can climb the world's highest mountain, then you too can also achieve your dreams. All you need is self-belief and a positive attitude." **TJ**

John O'Groats

Land's End

From Scotland to Cornwall

Tori was part of the team who travelled the famous journey from John O'Groats in Scotland (the UK's most northerly point) to Land's End in Cornwall (the UK's most southerly point) in a direct line.

- OVER 1,100 KM IN A DIRECT LINE
- TRAVELLED BY BIKE, KAYAK AND ON FOOT

Tori's adventures

- Cycled 2,400 km from one side of New Zealand to the other
- Skied 360 miles in freezing conditions to the North Pole

Tori and her kayak

Tori holds the World Record for the longest journey undertaken in open sea waters in Britain in a kayak, travelling from Cornwall to Pembrokeshire.

Gwendoline and Margaret Davies

Inspiring art collectors

What would you buy if you had £1? What about if you had £1,000 in your pocket? What if you had £69,000,000 in your bank account?

Luckily for the Davies sisters, Gwendoline and Margaret, their industrialist grandfather David Davies left them each £500,000 in his will. That's the equivalent of £69 million in today's money.

And how exactly did Gwendoline and Margaret spend this money? Well, the sisters became famous for collecting things. What did they love to collect?

ART!

Llandinam
GD 1882-1951
MD 1884-1963

For years the pair travelled through Europe, learning about art history in Germany and Italy and collecting art as they went.

The sisters' taste in art was timeless and they bought from young artists who later became famous and whose works now sell for millions of pounds – like Monet, Rodin and Turner.

They started collecting French Impressionist paintings and by 1924 the sisters had the largest collection of French Impressionist art in Britain.

And what did they do with this collection? They gave it to us.

True. Gwendoline and Margaret gave all their art to National Museum Wales in Cardiff. Thousands of people visit the collection every year.

The Beacon Light – JMW Turner

260+ artworks left to the Museum by the Davies sisters

The Gwendoline and Margaret Davies Charity is still giving out money to projects for young people involved in music or the arts.

Next time you are in Cardiff, why don't you go to see it? (Did I mention it's FREE?!) Why not take your sketch pad and pencils with you too? Who knows, maybe your artwork will be hanging in the museum in years to come!

World War I

During World War I (1914–1918) the sisters, who spoke fluent French, travelled to France to volunteer for the French Red Cross. They worked in a canteen, serving food and drink and looking after resting French soldiers. Gwendoline was even given a medal for her work.

FASCINATING FACT

Gwendoline and Margaret travelled around Europe in a chocolate-coloured Daimler car (very swish!)

1920

The sisters buy Gregynog Hall in Montgomeryshire, which becomes a centre for music and the arts in Wales.

VULCANA
(MIRIAM KATE WILLIAMS)

mystery (ooh!) 1874–1946

Victorian Superhero

As with all good superheroes, the exact details of where Kate was born are a bit of a mystery. She appears in the 1881 census in Aberdare and later in Abergavenny.

She was always different and grew into an extraordinary girl. People started to whisper about her strength and the buzz around her grew.

As a girl, she once saved two boys from drowning in the River Wye. Another time she stopped a horse running wild through the streets of Bristol, and she singlehandedly moved her school organ – to the shock of her teacher.

She was strong – so strong!

As a teenager she caught the eye of local bodybuilder William Hedley Roberts. He did shows, performing strongman tricks under the name of Atlas. When organising a performance in Pontypool, one of his acts got ill. Who should he get to fill the gap and save the day? Well, Kate, of course. Thus, 'Vulcana' was born in 1892.

Parlez-vous français?

The French adored Vulcana and she graced the cover of dozens of magazines.

VULCANA'S ADVICE FOR GIRLS

- Climb trees
- Exercise
- Be a tomboy

SHE DID WHAT?

- Lifted 25 kg with each arm ✓
- Raised a 12-stone man above her head ✓
- Won 100+ medals in weightlifting competitions ✓
- Wrestled at Bristol Circus and threw a man over her head ✓
- Singlehandedly raised a tipped vegetable cart in Covent Garden ✓
- Rushed into a burning building to save trapped horses ✓

OOPS!

Vulcana once floored a thief who tried to steal her purse. She carried him down the street over her shoulder to the local police station. What a woman!

Scandal Alert!!

Atlas and Vulcana hid a big secret - they weren't married. William already had a wife back in Wales. This was a big thing in Victorian times. They pretended they were brother and sister but had six children, who performed alongside them in the shows.

The Atlas and Vulcana show wowed audiences across Britain, Europe and even as far as Australia. Vulcana was so different to other women of her time. Audiences loved her and so did William.

They continued to amaze audiences with their incredible feats of strength until 1932. Vulcana died in 1946, but her influence remains today.

In Australia the Vulcana Circus' Vulcademy teaches circus tricks for women. Its slogan is 'home of the brave, strong and daring'.

A fitting tribute to an extraordinary woman.

COME TO SEE THE REMARKABLE SHOW:

ATLAS AND VULCANA!

DON'T TRY THIS AT HOME!

Vulcana's big trick was called The Tomb of Hercules. She would do a crab, supporting a platform with two horses and Atlas on top of her belly. Ouch!

ANN PETITT

Lancashire, England 1947–

Peace campaigner

Ann Pettitt loved her new home in the Welsh countryside. Here in Carmarthenshire was a chance for a quiet, simple life away from the hubbub of the city. But it would not be simple for long.

As a young mother, Ann worried about the Cold War, especially as 96 nuclear missiles were to be stored at a US military camp called Greenham Common near Newbury in England.

Ann felt something had to be done – but what?

Ann and some friends organised a march of over 120 miles from Cardiff to Greenham, in a hot and sweaty August in 1981. Their aim was to get rid of the missiles and protest nuclear war.

Did you know?

In 1982 Ann and a group of fellow protestors were invited over to speak to politicians in Moscow at a time where tensions between Russia and the West were high.

They arrived at the base gates on 5th September. They needed to get the attention of the newspapers, and the march was not enough. So what could the group do next?

They set up a camp. If the missiles stayed so, would they. Little did they know that their protest would last over 19 years. They slept under plastic sheets and knuckled down for a harsh winter, huddled around campfires.

In 1982 Greenham became a women-only protest – giving women around the world a voice to protest nuclear war. Newspapers started to take notice and so did other peace organisations. Packages started to arrive, one after another, including blankets, tents and food. The protest caught women's imaginations – soon other women joined, and the camp kept growing.

The 8-foot fence surrounding the base became a symbol of the protest. It kept the protestors out but it could not keep them quiet. Teddies were tied to it to symbolise the danger nuclear war posed to the children of the world. Women often chained themselves to it or held hands around the fence's 9-mile perimeter. It's estimated that 70,000 women protested at Greenham.

In 1991 the nuclear missiles were taken from the site – a victory for those who started, joined and continued the Greenham Common Protest.

Greenham Common's Peace Garden

Now a peace garden stands on the site, commemorating the protest. The flame statue in the middle represents the campfires, while the standing stones represent the women of Wales, including Ann, who started the iconic protest.

THE COLD WAR

A decades-long period of tension (1945–1991) between Western Europe/America and the Soviet Union/Eastern European countries. This never escalated into all-out war, but threatened to do so as tensions heightened, and in the 1980s governments and many people were seriously worried about a nuclear war.

PROTEST DIARIES

Ann's diaries from the protest are kept in the National Library of Wales.

Cranogwen
(Sarah Jane Rees)

Llangrannog 1839–1916

Sailor / Poet / Author / Teacher / Editor

Born with the sound of the sea in her ears, Sarah Jane Rees – Cranogwen – grew up in Llangrannog, a busy and bustling harbour village.

All the men in her family, including her brothers and sea captain father, worked on the sea. Cranogwen felt the sea call her too. Her mother had other plans and sent Cranogwen to work as a dressmaker in Cardigan. Ten days later she was back, begging her father to allow her to go to sea.

It seemed he had little choice.

Off she went and worked alongside him on his cargo ship, travelling back and forth to France. A woman working as a sailor was highly unusual. Some sailors even thought it was unlucky to have a woman on board ship. But Cranogwen thrived, and worked very hard to be seen as equal to – if not better than – any other sailor around her.

One stormy night near Strumble Head, their ship got into difficulty and was headed for the rocks. Cranogwen took charge of the ship and the men – they owed their lives to her quick thinking.

Studying in Liverpool and London, she gained a certificate as a master mariner – meaning she could command ships all over the world.

But she didn't want to sail the seas. Cranogwen wanted to go home.

She was a great sailor but a born teacher. In 1859 she opened a maritime school in Llangrannog. Hundreds of pupils were taught sailing and astronomy skills there by Cranogwen. They went on to sail the seven seas as captains themselves, proud to be known as Cranogwen's Captains – a true badge of honour.

SEXTANT

Cranogwen was highly skilled in using the stars to navigate a ship. This was an ancient skill, used for hundreds of years. She would have used a tool called a sextant, which measured the angles between two objects, like a star and the horizon, to help plot the ship's exact location. Ships use GPS today but sailors are still taught to navigate using the stars, just as Cranogwen would have taught her pupils in Llangrannog.

Cranogwen the poet

1865 — won a poetry prize at the National Eisteddfod – the first woman to do so

1870 — published a book of her poems and became a celebrity in Wales

A BROKEN HEART

Cranogwen's first girlfriend, Fanny Rees, died of tuberculosis (a disease of the lungs). Cranogwen was heartbroken. But she later met Jane Thomas, her partner for 20 years. Heart mended.

OUTSTANDING

Cranogwen has been called "the most outstanding Welsh woman of the 19th century" and her gravestone reads, "She stood on her own among the wives and women of our nation in genius and talent." A statue of Cranogwen by Sebastien Boyesen has been commissioned to stand on the clifftops of Llangrannog.

A FEISTY LADY

Cranogwen took her dog to chapel every Sunday, but nobody dared to tell her off.

ENDLESS TALENTS

- Sailor ✓
- Poet ✓
- Mathematician ✓
- Astronomer ✓
- Understood Latin ✓
- Teacher ✓
- Public Speaker ✓
- Magazine editor ✓
- Preacher ✓

Lowri Morgan

Presenter and ultra runner

Gowerton, Swansea
1975-

What makes a good runner? Strong heart, lungs and legs? How would a person with one leg longer than the other fare?

Believe it or not, Lowri Morgan – one of Wales' most famous runners – does have one leg shorter than the other. But it's never stopped her achieving. She's unstoppable.

Lowri can't remember a time when she wasn't running. Rugby was her first big love: she excelled but a painful leg injury (the reason one leg is shorter!) ended her rugby career. The injury was so serious doctors believed she'd never run again.

The news floored her. Lowri left the hospital in a wheelchair, not knowing what lay ahead, but she was determined: she would run again, someday.

After four long years of hard work, Lowri completed the New York Marathon (26 miles). She said goodbye to rugby – from now on running was her new passion, and many adventures lay ahead.

Over four years, Lowri ran a distance of 10,000 miles - the same as running from Wales to China and back!

CHALLENGE 1

Jungle Marathon

Where: Amazon rainforest, Brazil
Distance: 150 miles
Conditions: Temp 40°C/ Humidity 90%

With rivers to cross plus wild animals and poisonous plants, this is one of the most dangerous races in the world. Lowri ran against some of the world's toughest elite runners. The heat and exhaustion were unbearable and she even lost her toenails. To make matters worse, she was stung badly when she stepped on a hornets' nest. Lowri was so close to giving up, but she dug deep and made it to the finish in 10th place.

"When I can't sprint, I plod, but I never give up. I believe that attitude has helped me through life and some of the toughest races in the world." LM

MARATHON FOR BREAKFAST?

Most mornings Lowri runs 26 miles before you've even got out of bed!

"Running makes me happy."
— Lowri Morgan

CHALLENGE 2

6633 Ultra Marathon

Where: The Arctic
Distance: 350 miles
Conditions: Temp −40°c / Wind 70mph / 10 hours of daylight & 14 hours of darkness

Lowri has never shied away from a challenge, and this race would be challenging. Most runners don't make it to the finish line, failing to cover the 350 miles within the 8-day limit in freezing temperatures. In training, Lowri practised running in an industrial freezer to get used to the cold. No detail was overlooked: she practised getting into her sleeping bag in the dark, wearing thick gloves. This race was going to be tough.

The cold was biting. Even when she felt low, Lowri couldn't cry as the tears froze to her face.

Her mission was to reach the finish line. When the other runners slept, Lowri carried on running, going two days without sleep. In seven days, she slept a total of 12 hours (crazy!). She ran in near-darkness, with only the northern lights above her as company.

All the other runners dropped out, leaving Lowri alone to reach that finish line. Disaster struck when she broke a bone in her foot — but she still didn't quit. Even when she started hallucinating due to lack of sleep, she carried on.

Lowri crossed the finish line and won the race in 7 days and 38 minutes.

NATURE'S LIGHT SHOW

The Northern Lights are one of nature's most amazing shows. Appearing close to the north pole, the colourful lights appear to dance across the sky when tiny particles stream out of the sun and hit the earth's atmosphere. Recently they have even been seen in Wales!

47

MARY VAUGHAN

Teacher and creator of Sali Mali

"Children, would you like a story?" the class was asked by their kind teacher, Mary Vaughan Jones. The kids loved story time, especially when Miss Jones made up her own stories.

Mary was a talented teacher and she loved to write her own stories too. She started writing for a children's magazine and used her stories to entertain her class.

Mary taught in Aberystwyth in one of the first Welsh-language primary schools. Ysgol Gymraeg Aberystwyth was the first school of its kind. Today there are over 450 Welsh-medium primary schools in Wales.

In the 1950s, with more Welsh-language schools opening up, there was a need for more Welsh-language books for the pupils.

Using her talents for writing, Mary left teaching behind to become a full-time author.

In one story, one of her characters, Tomos Caradog, a mischievous little mouse, got ill. The young readers were so worried that they sent in get well cards for him.

Maenan, near Llanrwst
1918-1983

40+
The number of books Mary wrote

HAVE YOU EVER DRESSED UP AS ONE OF MARY'S CHARACTERS TO CELEBRATE WORLD BOOK DAY?

JONES

In 1969 Mary started writing a new series of books called *Darllen Stori* ('Read a Story') for beginners learning to read, and in that series we got to meet a bubbly girl in a bright orange dress: Sali Mali.

Sali also had friends, including Jac Do, Jac y Jwc and Nicw Nacw.

Hundreds of children learnt to read using Mary's books. They are still just as popular today, 50 years since they first came out.

As well as Welsh, the books are available in English, Spanish, German and Norwegian.

Mary died in 1983 – she never saw her books achieve worldwide success. But her characters still live on, with new authors creating new adventures for them.

Not many are familiar with Mary's name, but everybody knows Sali Mali.

PARTY! PARTY!

In 2019 Sali Mali turned 50. To mark the big birthday a lot of prominent buildings in Wales, like the Senedd, were lit up in bright orange.

MVJ Award

Every three years the Mary Vaughan Jones Prize is awarded to someone who's made an important contribution to children's literature in Wales. In 2012 it was awarded to Jac Jones, a wonderful author and illustrator who'd worked with Mary to create the look of Jac y Jwc, and Angharad Tomos won it in 2009.

15 — The animated adventures of Sali Mali can be seen in over 15 countries, and in languages like Telegu, Tamil and Arabic.

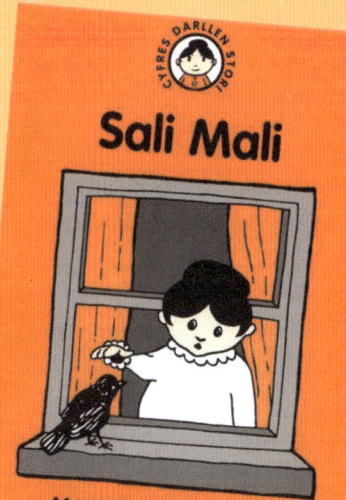

Mary adored Laurel and Hardy films from the 1930s. I wonder if this pair inspired Jac y Jwc?

RACHEL ROWLANDS

Founder of Rachel's Organic

Borth, Ceredigion 1946-

Winter 1982 – on her farm Brynllys in Ceredigion, Rachel Rowlands was in trouble.

Her husband, Gareth, was in hospital with a broken foot and Rachel had a dairy farm to manage and three kids to look after all by herself.

More trouble lay ahead. It started to snow and it did not stop. The whole of Wales lay under a thick, heavy blanket of snow. Strong winds created big snowdrifts up to three metres high and temperatures plunged to -20°C (brrrr, that's cold!).

Rachel had no water as the pipes had frozen, but what she did have was gallons and gallons of milk. But the milk lorry couldn't make it to the farm.

What could she do with the milk? Pouring it down the drain was not an option – Rachel had been brought up to not waste a thing.

Being resourceful, Rachel went to fetch her mother's butter-making kit and her grandmother's recipe book. She set about turning the milk into cream and butter and sold it to locals who couldn't reach the shops.

Everyone loved the produce and Rachel dived deeper into her grandmother's recipe book and started making yogurt from the Brynllys herd's milk to sell locally. Their brown and white Guernsey cows gave lovely thick, golden milk – perfect for delicious yogurt.

As the yogurt's popularity grew, Rachel and Gareth established Rachel's Organic. 10 years later, they opened a factory in Aberystwyth producing a range of yogurts, milk, butter, cream and rice pudding. Across the UK, Rachel's Organics pots hit the shelves in supermarkets and luxury hotels, and even on the Eurostar train to Paris.

Both Rachel and Gareth worked hard to develop the business and when they retired, they sold the company for £1.5 million. They returned to farming and the cows.

"I'm so proud that something that started as the result of trouble grew into an iconic brand." RR

Today Rachel's yogurts remain popular, and they are one of the most eco-friendly companies in the UK.

A single Guernsey cow can produce up to 6,000 litres of milk a year.

Reduce/Reuse/Recycle

Rachel's yogurt pots were the first in Britain to use 100% recycled plastic.

BRYNLLYS FARM
– leading the way

75 MILES
Milk used in Rachel's Organic yogurt comes from within 75 miles of the factory in Aberystwyth.

12,000 – the number of dairy farms in the UK

1.9 million – the number of dairy cows in the UK

Brynllys was the first organic dairy farm in the UK. Dinah, Rachel's mum, had a strong vision of how to treat the soil using natural methods.

Vitamin Sea
When she was little, Rachel would go down to the beach to pick seaweed to put on the farm fields. Seaweed is full of nutrients like potassium, zinc, iron and nitrogen, which help keep the soil healthy.

What a waste!
Over two million metric tonnes of plastic packaging waste is produced in the UK every year.

MARGARET HAIG THOMAS
2ND VISCOUNTESS RHONDDA

Raised in Llanwern
1883-1958

Suffragette

Margaret was born into a very rich family, an only child in a grand house full of servants. Margaret was a determined character. Like many women of her time, she was fed up with the inequality between men and women. They formed groups to campaign for the same rights as men.

Women able to vote in elections ✗

Women able to stand in elections ✗

Suffragette colours

Green = hope
White = purity
Violet = dignity
G+W+V = Give Women Votes!

She joined the Women's Social and Political Union under Emmeline Pankhurst and her daughters, Christabel and Sylvia. The group became known as suffragettes.

Margaret on the suffragette movement: "It gave us hope of freedom and power and opportunity."

Margaret organised meetings and rallies to get support for the cause. She gave speeches – but opponents threw rotten tomatoes and fish heads at her. She persisted.

The suffragettes started protesting more violently to get attention – Margaret too.

1910 – she broke away from a crowd and jumped into Prime Minister Asquith's car.

1913 – she firebombed a Royal Mail postbox in Newport and was sent to prison. There, like many other suffragettes, she went on hunger strike (refused to eat). The authorities freed her after six days so no suffragette would die for their cause.

Suffragette slogan:
"DEEDS NOT WORDS"

WHAT A WOMAN!

1. On the board of 33 companies
2. The woman with the highest salary in the UK
3. Set up *Time and Tide* magazine, with articles by famous authors

In 1914 World War I began and the suffragettes stopped protesting to concentrate on the war effort.

Margaret recruited women up and down the land for Women's National Service for Wales. Thousands upon thousands of women made weapons in factories, became nurses or worked in coal mines. Their loyal service showed that women could contribute as much as men. Margaret also went to America to persuade the President there to send weapons to Britain.

After the war ended in 1918, an Act of Parliament gave women over 30 the right to vote for the first time ever. 11 years later in 1928 (at last!) women were give the same voting rights as men.

Because of the actions of brave women like Margaret, women got more say in shaping the history of our nation.

Suffragette methods

- Disrupt parliamentary sessions
- Chain themselves to railings
- Smash windows
- Burn churches
- Hold mass protest rallies
- Attack politicians
- Set postboxes on fire
- Slash artwork at exhibitions
- Go on hunger strike

Queen Victoria on the suffragettes:

"Mad, wicked folly!"

Thanks, Vicky!

World 1sts

1893 – New Zealand gives women the vote

1906 – Finland lets women stand in elections

ANNIE ATKINS

Graphic designer extraordinaire

Dolwyddelan 1980–

At the end of every film the credits roll – the names of everyone that came together to make it, from movie stars and the director to the catering and lighting crew. One name you might see is Annie Atkins.

Annie was raised in a house full of love, art and creativity. Her parents were artists – her mam drew beautiful illustrations and her dad designed album covers for famous rock bands like Pink Floyd.

It was only natural that Annie became an artist too. She combined her visual communications degree with a film degree that led to her into the world of film and television.

To create a realistic world on screen, props like newspapers, letters, posters, etc. are created. Annie's job is to imagine, design and create these props.

Her first job was on a series called *The Tudors*, which followed the life of Henry VIII and his six wives. Annie even created the letter which King Henry signs in the series, ordering his wife Anne Boleyn's head to be chopped off!

Annie is a creative time-traveller – one minute she can be working on props for the 16th century, next Victorian London, post-war Germany, 1950s New York, or even realistic props for a country or place that does not exist.

She has a simple rule for her work: if recreating an item from history, she reproduces it how it would have been

Freeze frame! 95% of Annie's props only appear on the screen for seconds.

RUBBISH OR INSPIRATION?

Annie loves visiting charity and second-hand shops, looking at old letters and handwritten cards from different eras.

A graphic designer's work on a film:
- Create anything with lettering on it
- Create anything with a pattern on it
- Create anything with a picture on it
- Create anything made of paper

ANNIE'S WORKLOAD =
50% CREATED BY HAND
50% CREATED ON COMPUTER

SECRET CLUES

Annie sometimes sneaks the names of family and friends into her set designs, e.g. her goddaughter's name, Flo Sidaway, appears on a shop in Victorian London in the TV series Penny Dreadful.

done originally – by hand, by machine (like a printing press), or with a computer for more modern props.

From her studio in Dublin she designs items for some of the world's best directors, including Wes Anderson. As lead Graphic Designer on his film *The Grand Budapest Hotel*, she went to live on the set in Gorlitz in Germany as there was so much work to be done. The final film is a beautiful masterpiece.

Annie designed one of the film's iconic props: the pink Mendl's cake box with a bright blue bow. They now sell for hundreds of pounds.

One of the film's stars, Jeff Goldblum, called her "a master craftswoman – she makes the unreal seem hyperrreal... and utterly magical."

DID YOU KNOW?

Annie created and designed the fake newspapers and money used in the fictional country of Zubrowska in *The Grand Budapest Hotel*.

The 2015 Academy Award (Oscar) for Best Production Design was won by *The Grand Budapest Hotel* for their creativity and artistic vision.

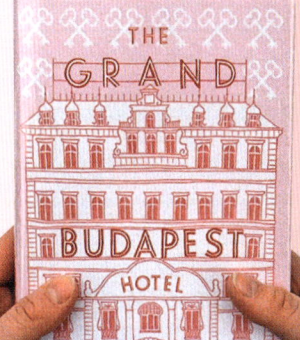

"I'm not brilliant at anything, I just know a little bit of everything and have learnt to cheat over the years."

ANNIE ATKINS

MARY QUANT

Fashion designer

Blackheath, London 1930–

"Mary!" came the shout from upstairs.

Young Mary knew why she was in trouble. Using her mother's sewing scissors, Mary had cut up her bedding to make clothes for her dolls. Yes, her love of fashion developed early.

Her parents, Jack and Mildred, were both originally from south Wales before moving to London as teachers. Mary has always considered herself Welsh.

Fashion was Mary's life, but Jack and Mildred worried that there was no future for her in it. So instead of fashion school she attended art college, but went to dressmaking classes in the evenings.

At Goldsmiths College she met and married Alexander Plunket Greene. They were perfect for one another. Mary was creative and Alex had a great head for business and marketing.

2009 Mary's miniskirt design is put on a stamp celebrating the Top 10 British designs of all time.

They combined their talents and opened a clothes shop called Bazaar on the very trendy King's Road in London.

Mary, aged only 25, designed and made easy-to-wear, simple clothes. She understood that as the Swinging Sixties started, girls didn't want to dress as mini versions of their mothers. They wanted to look and feel young and yearned for fresh, colourful, fun designs. New, exciting clothes for a new era.

Mary wanted the shop to be a success. She used the shop's profits to buy more fabric to make more dresses, sewing through the night to get new stock on the shop floor ready for opening time.

One of Mary's favourite models was fellow Welsh girl Grace Coddington from Anglesey. She had striking flaming red hair and became a fashion icon herself, as Creative Director of Vogue fashion magazine.

"The whole point of fashion is to make fashionable clothes available to everyone."
MARY QUANT

The miniskirt was named after the Mini Cooper car – another design icon from the 1960s.

Bazaar was a buzz of young customers, loud music and late nights. Even members of The Beatles, the world's most famous band, popped in to buy dresses for their girlfriends. George Harrison, the band's bass guitarist, even got married in clothes designed by Mary. Her influence was growing.

By 1967 it's estimated that 7 million women had something designed by Quant in their wardrobe.

But one piece became more iconic than any other – the miniskirt. During the Sixties, hemlines got higher and higher and Mary was called "the mother of the miniskirt". She in return said it was simply what her customers asked for.

The miniskirt became a fashion statement for the Swinging Sixties. Mary even got a medal from the Queen — although the Pope was not a fan and called the skirt "indecent" (you can't make everyone happy, right?!).

A blue plaque sits on the wall of 88 King's Road, showing where Bazaar was.

A style trailblazer, modern fashion owes so much to her. Almost 500,000 people visited an exhibition of her designs held at the Victoria and Albert Museum in 2019. Her clothes look as fresh today as they did on the Bazaar shop floor 60 years ago.

LONDON TOO FAR? NO PROBLEM!

Customers who couldn't make it to Bazaar could order patterns for Mary's designs to sew themselves. There was also a range of designs for Daisy – a doll, marketed as 'the most fashionable doll in the world'.

DID YOU KNOW?
Mary helped make the duvet popular in the UK. Think of her tonight as you snuggle into your cosy bed!

SHIRLEY BASSEY

World-famous songstress from Tiger Bay

Cardiff 1937–

A little girl sings as she sweeps her front doorstep and her neighbours smile.

Her brothers and sisters, on the other hand, complain that she never stops singing – even getting banned from the school choir for singing too loudly does not stop her.

Would her school choir master have imagined that Shirley Bassey would still be entertaining huge audiences today, at 85 years old?

Originally from Tiger Bay in Cardiff, Shirley left school at 14 to pack saucepans in a factory. Her father had left when she was only 2, so the family struggled, but love and hard work kept them together.

Shirley always had big dreams. She dreamed of being a fashion model – wearing glamorous new clothes instead of her sisters' hand-me-downs.

After work at the factory, she sang in pubs and clubs around Tiger Bay. Her voice was dramatic, passionate and emotional and people really loved listening to her.

In 1953 she won a recording contract which took her to stages in London, New York and Las Vegas, and as her records sold, she gained worldwide fame. She sang the theme tunes for James Bond films, including *Diamonds Are Forever* and *Goldfinger*.

Because of her amazing voice, Shirley has sung in some of the most famous venues in the world.

NURSE SHIRLEY

Shirley intended to become a nurse but had one problem – she can't stand the sight of blood.

For the first time in her life, she could not sing. It took months with a voice coach for the famous voice to return.

In 1999, with a worldwide audience watching, she opened the Rugby World Cup tournament in Cardiff. She sang with passion in a wonderful Welsh flag dress.

Her voice remains as iconic as Shirley herself, entertaining audiences worldwide for 70 years.

"I've never had a singing lesson... I can't read music. My voice is there!" (points to her heart)

SHIRLEY BASSEY

When she recorded *Goldfinger*, the song's last note was so long that she fainted!

Shirley performs all over the world and is known for being glamorous, in dresses of feathers and sequins.

But life has not always been easy. When her daughter Samantha died, Shirley was inconsolable with grief.

DAME SHIRLEY BASSEY WAY

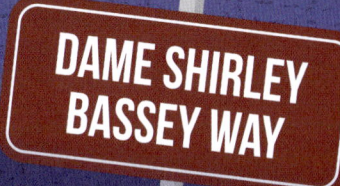

The road outside Noah's Ark Hospital in Cardiff was renamed to recognise her contribution to the charity.

70 YEARS OF PERFORMING
105 SINGLES
70 ALBUMS
140 MILLION RECORDS SOLD

PUFF-PUFF-PUFF

A carriage on the Snowdon Mountain Railway is named after her.

SHIRLEY BASSEY

Glamour at Glasto

Shirley sang at Glastonbury aged 70, wearing diamond-encrusted wellingtons with her initials on them.

LUCY THOMAS

The mother of Wales' coal industry

Llansamlet 1781-1847

Can you imagine going through life not being able to read or write? I can't. Like most of the population at the time, Lucy Thomas could not read or write. Despite this, she became one of the most successful and influential industrialists of the age. Let's take a look at her incredible life.

To begin we need to step back to 1833 – Lucy's husband Robert died, leaving her a widow with eight children to feed, clothe and raise.

Robert owned a coal mine (Waun Wyllt) near Merthyr Tydfil: a small mine with little output. During this period, women were not involved in business. They did not run coal mines. But Lucy did – taking the big step of taking over the leadership at Waun Wyllt.

With Lucy in charge the mine grew, especially when they discovered a rich vein of the best quality of coal.

LEARN MORE!

Visit the Big Pit National Coal Museum in Blaenavon to see what life was like underground.

X for Lucy

Papers in the Glamorgan Archive show that like many illiterate people, Lucy signed with an X.

1906
A decorative water fountain was built on Merthyr High Street in memory of Lucy and Robert.

1913
Barry in South Wales became the world's biggest port, sending coal to the four corners of the world.

Lucy reached out and struck a great deal with coal wholesalers from London. Coal from Wales became known worldwide for its impressive quality. Coal from Wales was sent all around the world and the industry exploded, with hundreds of mines set up. Coal was king.

Waun Wyllt became over ten times more successful under her care. But not everyone was impressed by Lucy and her extraordinary business skills. The Coal Exchange in Cardiff refused her entry because she was female. Indignantly she sent them a note which read: "My coal is equal to any man's!"

They begrudgingly let her in, and she was formidable.

For 14 years she nurtured the business, until she died suddenly of typhoid fever in 1847.

In an era when men, and only men, led businesses, Lucy brought attention and acclaim to one of Wales' most important industries and shaped the history of our nation.

WHY WAS WELSH COAL BEST?

- Burnt very hot
- Made less ash

£1,000
WAUN WYLLT'S VALUE UNDER ROBERT

£11,000
WAUN WYLLT'S VALUE UNDER LUCY
(Approx £1,215,928.45 in today's money)

MEENA UPADHYAYA

Scientist and genetics researcher

Delhi, India 1948–

Meena's story starts over 4,000 miles away from Wales – she was born in Delhi, India.

Not long after 18-year-old Meena's wedding to Krishna, the young couple left India to set up home here, settling in Cardiff in the 1970s.

Meena thought she'd work in a shop, but Krishna knew his new wife was a remarkably talented scientist and encouraged her to study. She completed a Master of Science at the University of Edinburgh followed by a doctorate at Cardiff University.

They loved life in Cardiff. They worked hard and soon welcomed their daughter, Rachna. Weekends were spent visiting the city's many parks and life was a joy.

But the family was devastated when Krishna died suddenly, aged 35. Meena's family begged her to return to India, but she knew that she and Rachna belonged in Cardiff.

After Krishna's death, Meena threw herself into her research. She spent her career focusing on genetic disorders, developing pioneering tests to aid in the diagnosis of more than 20 different genetic diseases. She knew her research was making a difference to the lives of thousands of sufferers of little-known diseases.

But Meena sometimes struggled to get recognition for her work. Visitors to her lab at Cardiff University sometimes mistook her for the tea lady. She was the only one in her labs wearing a sari.

Genetic traits you inherit:
- eye colour
- height
- shoe size

And thousands of others too!

YOU'VE GOT A FRIEND

Some experiments took over 18 hours to complete and Meena's friends helped to look after Rachna.

Some diseases get passed down from one generation to the next – these are called genetic diseases.

SNAP!

Identical twins have the same DNA. There are around 40 million identical twins in the world. Benin in Africa has the highest rate of identical twin births.

"I've had multiple barriers because of my religion, my language, my physical attributes and my beliefs." MU

But Meena used these experiences to create something positive. She set up the Ethnic Minority Welsh Women Achievement Association, shining a light on women contributing to many areas in Wales, including arts, business, technology and science.

Although now retired, her groundbreaking research has a big effect on the lives of people worldwide, leading to the development of treatments and hopes of healthier lives.

DID YOU KNOW?

DNA can help catch criminals. Scientists can help trace culprits due to the DNA they leave behind at crime scenes.

DAD & MAM, GRANDMA & GRANDPA

50% / 50%

Everyone inherits 50% of their DNA from their dad and 50% from their mum. They in turn get their DNA from their parents.

In the 1800s several generations of a family in America were born blue because of a rare genetic condition.

"One should never give up. If you set your mind on doing something – you can do it."

MEENA UPADHYAYA

GLOSSARY

BILINGUAL
Written in or speaking two languages. In Wales, most bilingual people speak Welsh and English.

CARGO
A cargo ship carries goods, not people.

CENSUS
Every 10 years there is a massive survey of everyone living in the UK. On an appointed night each family notes who is living in their household, including names, ages, work and how they're related to each other. This information is used to plan public services in your area but kept secret from the public for 100 years. An incredibly important document for future historians.

INDUSTRIALIST
A person involved in the ownership or management of an industry such as coal or slate mining.

GRAPHIC DESIGNER
Graphic designers use colour, fonts and images to design things like signs, posters, books, etc. This book was designed by a graphic designer!

CONCENTRATION CAMP
A place in which large numbers of people are held as prisoners for political reasons. Unlike real prisons, people are not there because they did anything wrong. Instead, they are members of a group that a government wishes to punish or control.

IMPRESSIONIST ART
Begun in France in the 1860s by a group of rebellious young artists who wanted to introduce a new kind of painting – capturing a moment in time using colour and light.

DNA
Deoxyribonucleic acid

INEQUALITY
Inequality is when people don't respect the differences between people, and don't treat everyone fairly, regardless of race, gender, age, disability, religion or sexual preference.

TAX
The money a government (people who run the country) collects to pay for services like schools, roads, street lights, the police, hospitals and so on.

ACTIVITIES

HOW TO BE WONDROUS IN 5 EASY STEPS

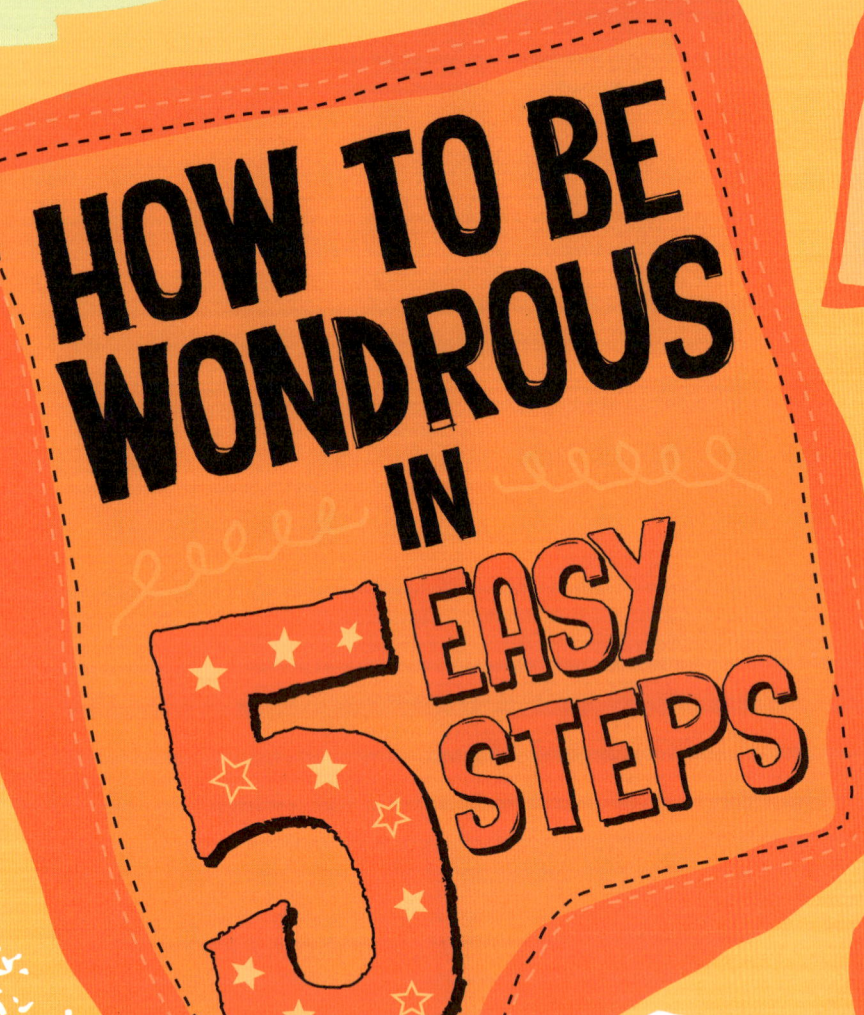

1. JOIN THE SCHOOL COUNCIL
A great way to give your opinion and improve your school.

2. SPONSOR A GIRL
Not everyone is given the same opportunities in this world, especially in education. Why not sponsor a girl? You can share letters and learn about each other's lives.

Visit ActionAid or World Vision for more info.

3. READ
Here's a little secret: reading is the quickest, cheapest way to travel round the world. You can meet so many characters and go back in time without leaving your bedroom. Check out your local library.

4. KEEP A DIARY
You don't have to write a lot - just a couple of sentences about your day: what you did, how you feel. Looking back 20 years from now, you can see the journey you've been on.

5. JOIN A CLUB
Why not try something new? Karate, squash, rugby, football, baking, dancing, sewing - the possibilities are endless. Go online to find out what clubs are in your area.

BE WONDROUS!

Hello, you!

Welcome to the Wondrous Women of Wales Club. As a new member, we need to get to know you. Fill in your details.

Name:

Age:

Brothers or sisters?

Pet?

School:

Best toy:

Year:

Favourite food:

Teacher:

What makes you laugh out loud?

Your besties:

Hidden skills:

Be wondrous!

How are you going to change the world? Dream big or small – use this space to write your dreams and wishes for the future.

In the future I'm going to...

WORD SEARCH

F	A	B	P	E	R	I	G	I	Q	O	H	N	H	O	G	T	U
G	A	E	C	E	R	M	E	N	G	R	A	P	H	I	C	S	P
T	K	S	G	U	U	J	N	D	W	Q	Z	X	A	I	T	E	A
B	R	N	H	M	H	R	E	Y	M	A	R	T	D	H	L	T	U
S	I	U	X	I	O	R	T	S	C	I	H	T	A	A	H	O	L
S	T	I	G	T	O	S	I	K	Q	N	T	P	O	Q	L	R	V
E	E	A	C	O	T	N	C	X	O	L	E	C	K	X	W	P	R
S	V	O	R	H	Y	M	S	H	A	S	A	O	I	R	U	O	E
R	D	E	M	G	N	Y	T	U	N	V	C	R	Y	G	A	L	K
Q	C	K	R	Y	A	A	V	E	E	D	H	Z	S	L	A	J	A
E	L	I	S	E	R	Z	O	C	S	T	E	X	C	M	K	R	E
W	H	N	R	A	S	A	I	U	T	Y	R	D	R	M	J	H	R
R	A	J	M	U	L	T	K	N	G	F	M	E	D	I	V	U	B
S	A	L	I	M	A	L	I	V	G	C	I	M	U	M	M	Y	E
D	N	W	E	I	G	H	T	L	I	F	T	E	R	X	X	D	D
L	P	A	T	Z	E	R	N	O	D	N	O	W	K	E	A	T	O
A	D	V	E	N	T	U	R	E	E	N	O	I	D	Y	W	G	C

- Adventure
- Art
- Cigar
- Coal
- Codebreaker
- Doctor
- Everest
- Fashion
- Genetics
- Graphic
- Marathon
- Mummy
- Protest
- Sali Mali
- Singer
- Stargazing
- Taekwondo
- Teacher
- Weightlifter
- Yogurt

JADE JONES

START

Can you help Jade find her way through the maze to reach the gold medal?

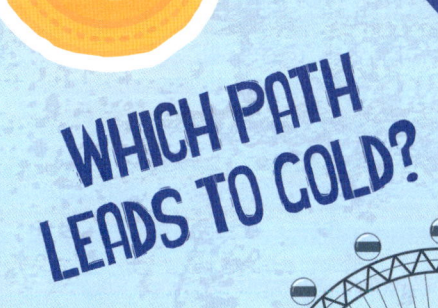

WHICH PATH LEADS TO GOLD?

KATE BOSSE-GRIFFITHS

Which of these Egyptian scarab beetles is different to the others? After finding it, what about colouring them in?

SCARAB BEETLE

Ancient Egyptian art was full of symbols. One of them was the scarab beetle. The beetle symbolised rebirth and was seen as lucky. Archaeologists in Egypt have found colourful images of the beetle on art, letters and valuable jewellery, and even inside some mummies.

Angharad Tomos

Angharad Tomos was inspired by Anne Frank to keep a diary.
Writing in one every day will help you to improve your writing skills!
What can you write about today?

Today I...

Gwendoline and Margaret Davies

Anyone can be a wondrous woman – they are around us every day. Why not draw a picture of a wondrous woman who inspires you?

Inspiration:

- one of the women in this book
- your mam / sister / auntie / nan
- your teacher
- someone famous

TORI JAMES

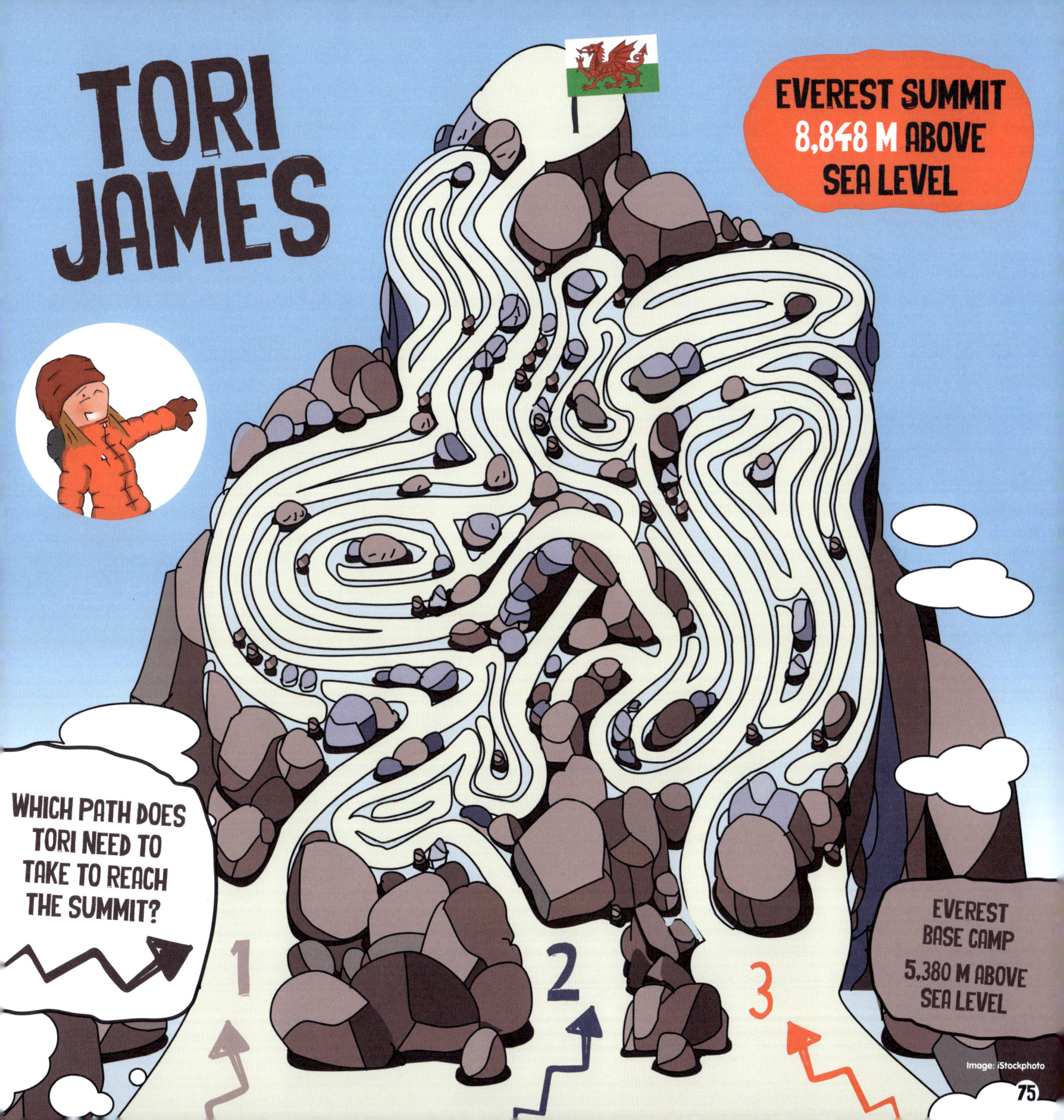

EVEREST SUMMIT 8,848 M ABOVE SEA LEVEL

WHICH PATH DOES TORI NEED TO TAKE TO REACH THE SUMMIT?

1   2   3

EVEREST BASE CAMP 5,380 M ABOVE SEA LEVEL

MAIR RUSSELL JONES

TOP SECRET

An urgent coded message has been intercepted by Station X. Can you crack the code using this key?

Coded Letter	A	B	C	D	E	F
Answer	L	K	J	I	H	G

Coded Letter	G	H	I	J	K	L
Answer	X	W	V	U	T	S

Coded Letter	M	N	O	P	Q	R
Answer	F	E	D	C	B	A

Coded Letter	S	T	U	V	W	X
Answer	Y	Z	R	Q	P	O

Coded Letter	Y	Z
Answer	M	N

Secret Message

UNRO QXXBL. QN BDZO. ERIN MJZ.

RACHEL ROWLANDS

It's milking time at Brynllys Farm in Ceredigion. But oh no, one of Rachel's dairy cows is missing. How can Rachel get through the maze to the lost cow?

START

WHAT'S YOUR FAVOURITE YOGURT FLAVOUR?

MARY QUANT

You've joined Mary's design team at Bazaar. Your task is to design two new dresses for the shop.

DETECTIVE TASK

Go online and search for photos of Mary Quant's designs. Which one would you like to wear?

MARY LOVES

- STRONG COLOURS
- GEOMETRIC SHAPES
- PETER PAN COLLARS
- SHORT HEMLINES

LOWRI MORGAN

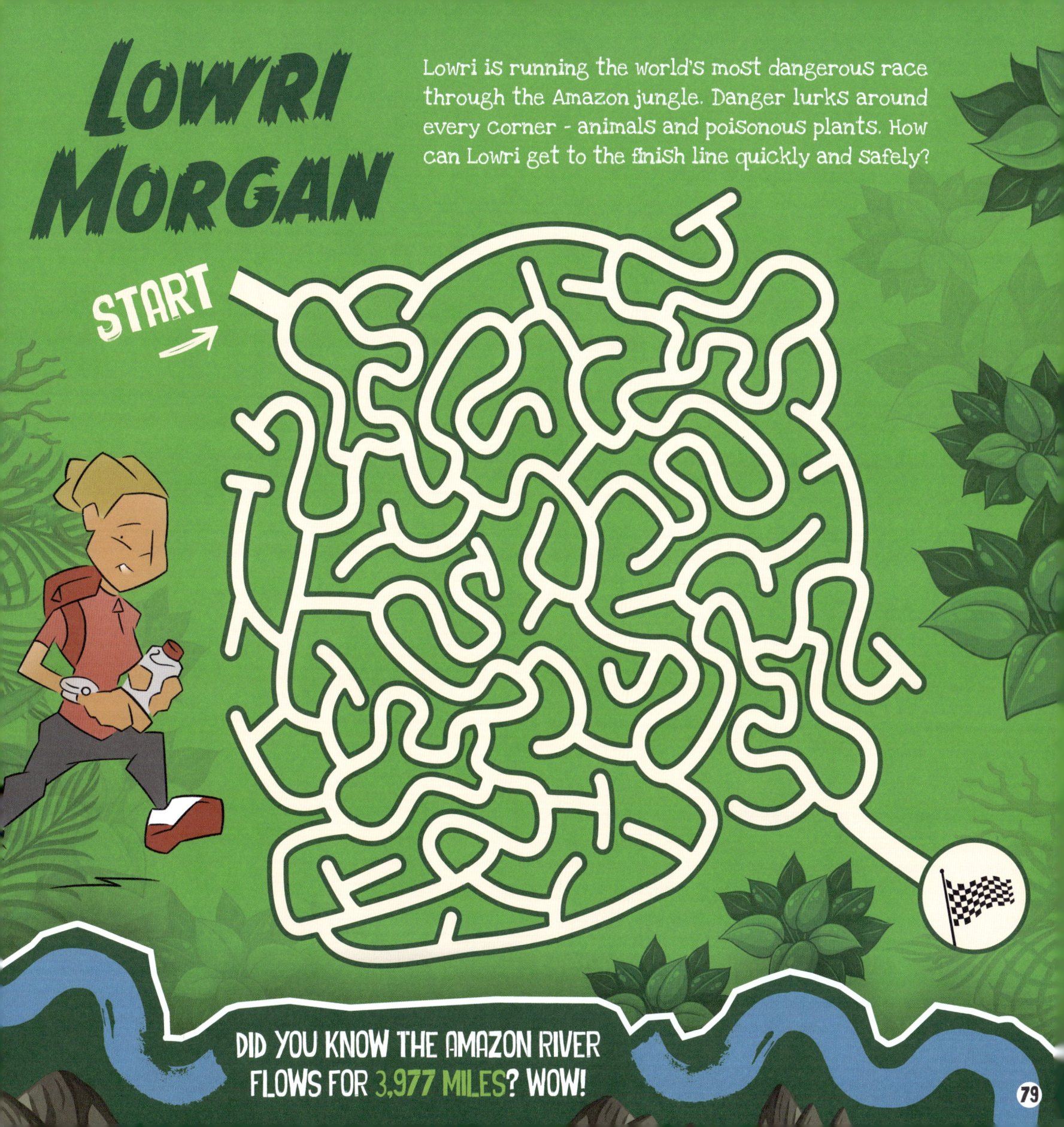

Lowri is running the world's most dangerous race through the Amazon jungle. Danger lurks around every corner - animals and poisonous plants. How can Lowri get to the finish line quickly and safely?

START

DID YOU KNOW THE AMAZON RIVER FLOWS FOR 3,977 MILES? WOW!

ANNIE ATKINS

Great news! Annie is the chief Graphic Designer on a new film and she needs your help to make the imaginative, creative and colourful props.

Help Annie design fake money for the film.

Questions

- What's the name of your made-up country?

- Money usually has a picture of the country's leader or native animals/plants printed on it. Who or what will appear on your currency?

- What is the symbol for your money? It's £ in Wales, $ in the USA or € in Europe.

- How colourful will your design be?

DETECTIVE TASK

Go to annieatkins.com to see examples of Annie's work or raid your piggy bank to look at some real money.

Cranogwen

Welcome to Cranogwen's maritime school. Here's your task, set by your headmistress herself. You'll need an adult, a warm coat and a dark sky outside to complete the task.

WHAT SHAPE IS THE MOON TONIGHT?

- New moon (no moon showing) ☐
- Waxing crescent ☐
- First quarter ☐
- Waxing gibbous ☐
- Full moon ☐
- Waning gibbous ☐
- Last quarter ☐
- Waning crescent ☐

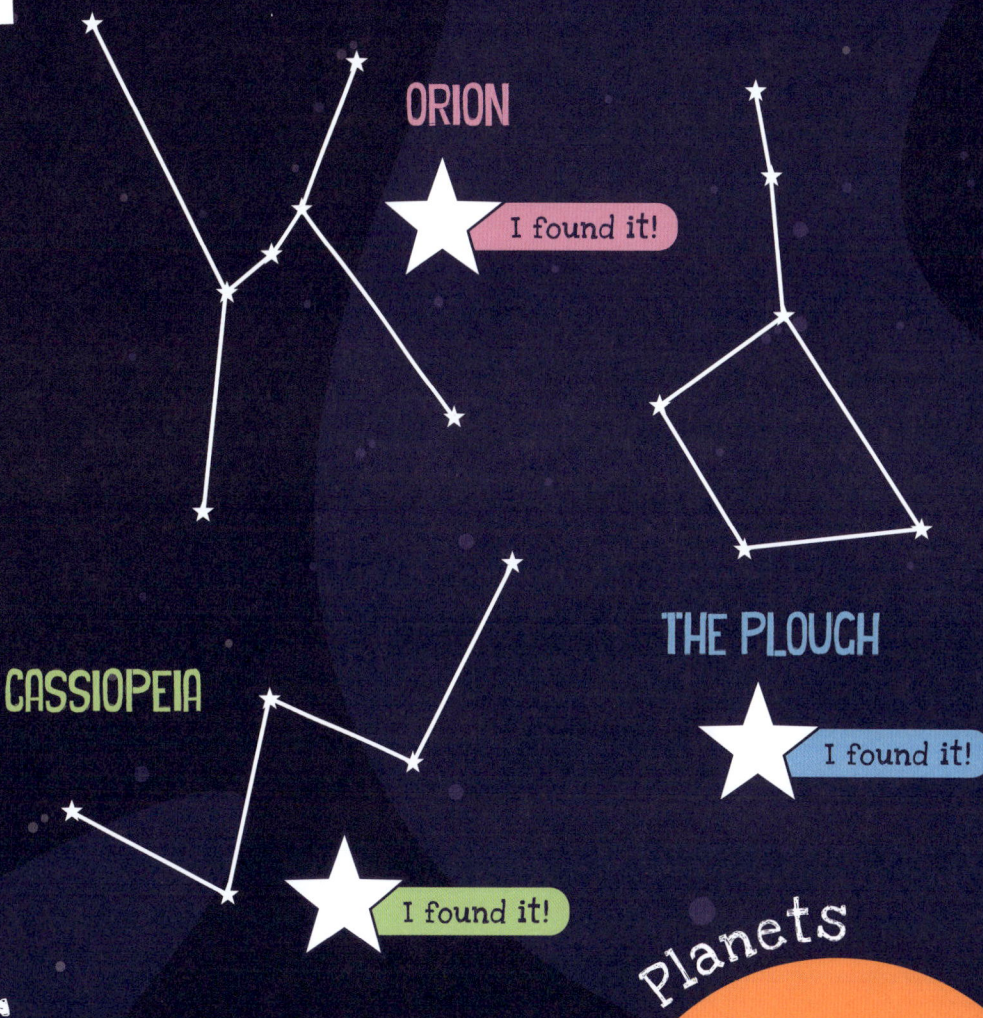

ORION — I found it!

CASSIOPEIA — I found it!

THE PLOUGH — I found it!

DETECTIVE TASK

Go online to find out when the International Space Station will next fly over where you live.

Tips

- Winter is the best time of year to see the stars, as it gets dark earlier.
- National Parks in Wales are great for stargazing. Look out for Dark Sky signs, which mean that light-pollution levels are low and the stars are easier to see.

Planets

Some planets, like Venus, are easier to spot than stars. Venus is incredibly bright and is the first 'star' to appear in the night sky and the last to disappear in the morning.

PROTEST!

ANNE PETTITT

Ann Pettitt, Eileen Beasley and Margaret Haig Thomas all protested for what they believed in. Lots of newspaper articles were written about each of them.

Your task is to create a newspaper article about one of these protests, or something close to your own heart.

Headline here (something catchy)

Your story (go for it!)

MARGARET HAIG THOMAS

EILEEN BEASLEY

MEENA UPADHYAYA

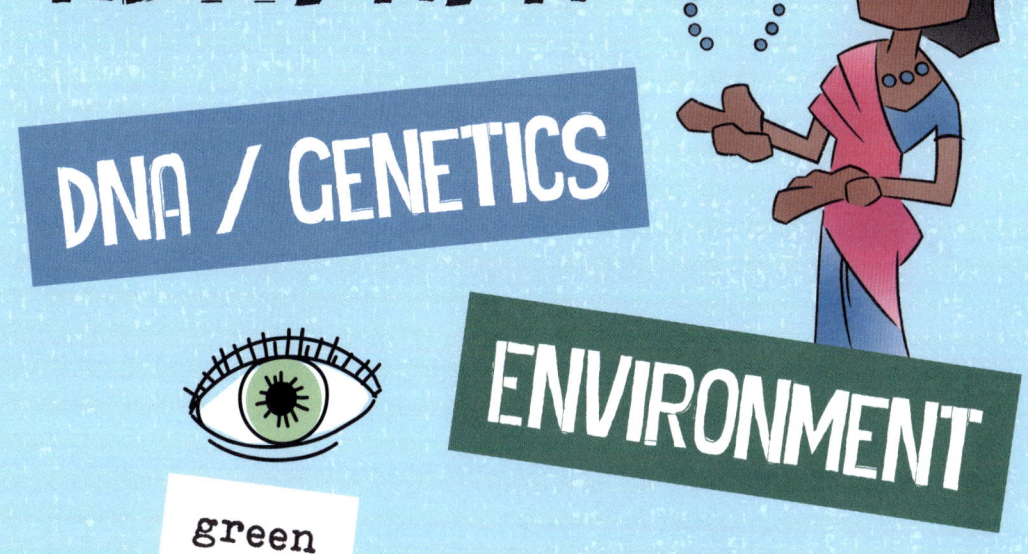

DNA gives us many of our traits, but the environment we grow up and live in affects us too.

What causes these traits – DNA/genetics or the environment? Draw a line to the correct category.

DNA / GENETICS

ENVIRONMENT

- green eyes
- write with your left hand
- height
- hate pop music
- freckles
- love shopping
- blood group
- speak Welsh

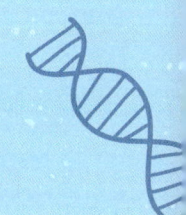

Answers:

DNA – write with your left hand, green eyes, blood group, freckles, height
Environment – hate pop music, speak Welsh, love shopping

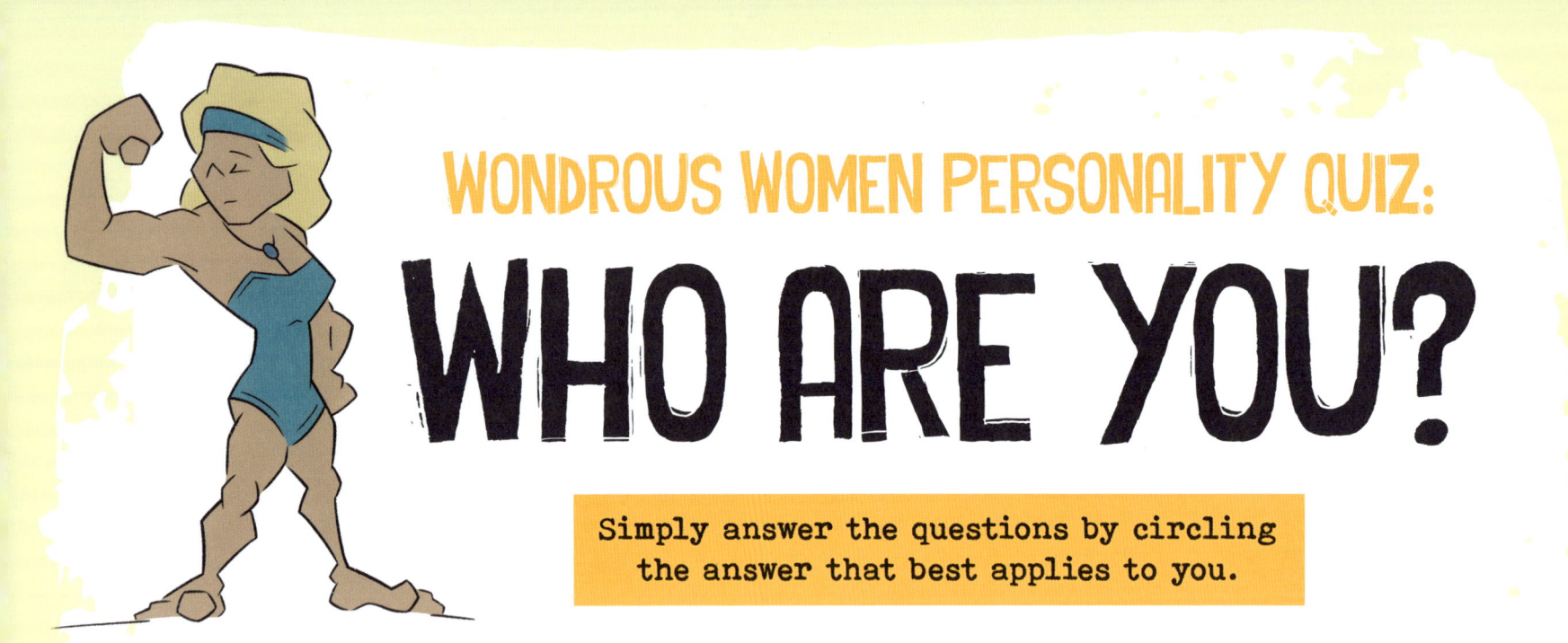

WONDROUS WOMEN PERSONALITY QUIZ: WHO ARE YOU?

Simply answer the questions by circling the answer that best applies to you.

QUESTION 1

What's your favourite subject at school?

A Art – I love painting
B Shh! I really don't like school
C I like being home on the farm
D Science – experiments are the best
E Geography – researching locations for an adventure

QUESTION 2

How would your friends describe you?

A Creative – I'm always drawing
B Like a bird – always singing
C I'm a problem solver – very inventive
D Very patient – always ready for hard work
E Energetic – always on the go

QUESTION 3

Where do you see yourself in 20 years?

A   In a city, surrounded by history and creative people
B   Somewhere very glamorous
C   There's no place like home
D   Wherever my work and family take me
E   Up a mountain, probably

QUESTION 4

What sort of work would you like?

A   Something visual, using my imagination
B   On stage, entertaining an audience
C   Running my own business
D   In a laboratory, doing experiments
E   Anything adventurous – I love a challenge

QUESTION 5

How are you going to make your mark?

A   Creating beautiful, inspirational artwork
B   Leaving an audience wanting more
C   Pleasing customers with great products
D   Helping others through my scientific research
E   Setting challenges and breaking records

Turn the page to discover your identity.

WONDROUS WOMEN PERSONALITY QUIZ RESULTS

A MAINLY A - You're the new Annie Atkins
You're creative, imaginative and love researching and making things. Maybe Annie has a space for you in her Dublin studio!

B MAINLY B - You're a young Shirley Bassey
Watch out Shirley – a new songstress is ready to take to the stage, with a selection of wonderful costumes. Audiences around the world are bound to fall in love with you.

C MAINLY C - You're Rachel Rowlands' apprentice
The business world is calling you – make your mark and run an internationally renowned company. You'll travel around the world but in your heart, there is no place like home.

D MAINLY D - You're Meena Upadhyaya's new lab partner
Laboratories are your stomping ground and you know that your work is making a difference. You break down barriers that stop you being the best.

E MAINLY E - Adventurer extraordinaire like Tori James
You are brave, determined and ready to face any challenge. Get your backpack – adventure lies just beyond the horizon.

ASK THE AUTHOR

Medi Jones-Jackson answers readers' questions!

1. What was the inspiration behind the book?
(Efa & Cadi Jones, Cardiff)

I read loads of books to my daughter Anest about amazing women from all over the world, like Simone Biles, Malala Yousafzai and Greta Thunberg, and I thought there ought to be a book about great women from Wales. What better way was there of seeing a book like that in the shops than to write it myself?

2. Why aren't there photographs of the women in the book?
(Greta Grug, Aberystwyth)

Interesting question. From the very start, while working out what the book would be like, I didn't want real pictures of the women. Photos exist of some of them but not of others. For me, their talent and their stories are important, not what they look like. But you can search for photos online. Are they similar to the cartoon? Do they look like you thought they would?

3. Where do the facts come from?
(Lili Green, Ruthin)

I really love bizarre facts and general knowledge and I'm really interested in women's history. I spend weeks reading books and newspaper articles and hunting out interviews with the women. The internet is a brilliant resource and it would have been very hard to write *Wondrous Women of Wales* without it.

4. Have you got a favourite Wondrous Woman?
(Anest Jackson, Bow Street)

It's so hard to choose! I love how determined Frances Hoggan was to make her dream of being a doctor come true. Why do people in Wales not talk about her more? Vulcana is a really interesting figure, and very unusual for the period she lived in, and I must confess that I love Anne Atkins' design work.

WWoW Timeline

- **1781** — Lucy Thomas is born
- **1789** — Betsi Cadwaladr is born 
- **1833** — Lucy Thomas starts running Waun Wyllt coal mine
- **1839** — Sarah Jane Rees (Cranogwen) is born 
- **1843** — Frances Hoggan is born 
- **1845** — Amy Dillwyn is born 
- **1854** — Betsi Cadwaladr travels to the Crimea
- **1859** — Cranogwen opens her maritime school in Llangrannog  
- **1865** — Cranogwen's poetry wins an award at the National Eisteddfod
- **1870** — Frances Hoggan becomes a doctor

Gwendoline Davies is born

Margaret Davies is born

Kate Bosse-Griffiths is born

Gwendoline and Margaret Davies travel to France to help during WWI

Mary Vaughan Jones is born and women over 30 win the right to vote

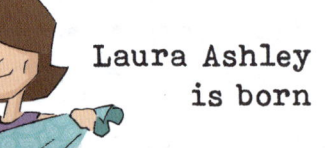

Laura Ashley is born

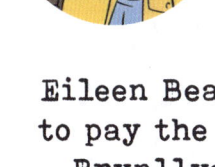

- **1874** — Miriam Kate Williams (Vulcana) is born
- **1882**
- **1883** — Margaret Haig Thomas is born 
- **1884**
- **1892** — Vulcana performs her first show with Atlas
- **1910**
- **1913** — Margaret Haig Thomas is sent to prison for firebombing a postbox
- **1914**
- **1917** — Mair Russell Jones is born
- **1918**
- **1921** — Eileen Beasley is born 
- **1925**
- Betty Campbell is born
- Shirley Bassey is born and Kate Bosse-Griffiths leaves Nazi Germany 
- Mair Russell Jones starts working at Bletchley Park 
- Ann Pettitt is born
- Eileen Beasley refuses to pay the tax bill and Brynllys Farm is the first certified organic dairy farm in the UK 
- Angharad Tomos is born 
- **1930** — Mary Quant is born 
- **1934**
- **1937**
- **1939**
- **1941** — Ysgol Gymraeg Aberystwyth, the first Welsh-language primary school, is established
- **1946** — Rachel Rowlands is born 
- **1947**
- **1948** — Meena Upadhyaya is born 
- **1952**
- **1955** — Mary Quant's shop Bazaar opens on the King's Road, London
- **1958**
- **1959** — Shirley Bassey becomes the first Welsh artist to have a No.1 single

89

1960 — Eileen Beasley receives a tax bill in Welsh and Betty Campbell starts teacher training

1962 — The first Laura Ashley shop opens in Machynlleth

THIS BUILDING WAS THE LOCATION OF LAURA ASHLEY'S FIRST SHOP

Rachel's Organic is established

1963 — Mary Quant wins the Dress of the Year award

Jade Jones is born

1966 — Gareth and Rachel Rowlands take over Brynllys Farm

Shirley Bassey opens the Rugby World Cup tournament in Cardiff

1969 — The first Sali Mali book is published

1975 — Lowri Morgan is born

Greenham Common Peace Garden opens

1979 — Haley Gomez is born

1980 — Annie Atkins is born

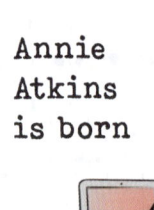

Mair Russell Jones finally decides to talk about working at Bletchley Park

1981 — Tori James is born and Ann Pettitt marches to Greenham Common

1983 — The first book in the *Rwdlan* series is published

1984	
1991	Nuclear weapons leave Greenham Common
1993	
1998	Nelson Mandela visits Betty Campbell in Cardiff
1999	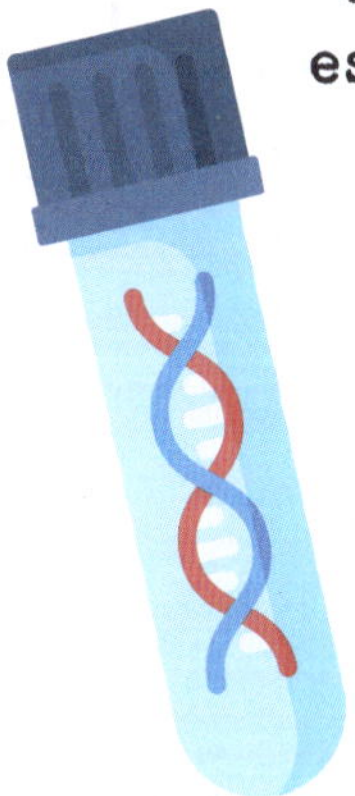
2000	Meena Upadhyaya completes a fellowship with the Royal College of Pathologists and the last protestors leave Greenham Common
2002	
2007	Tori James reaches the summit of Everest
2008	
2009	Lowri Morgan runs the Amazon Jungle Marathon and Mary Quant's miniskirt features on a stamp

	Lowri Morgan wins the Arctic ultra marathon
2011	
2012	Jade Jones wins her first Olympic gold medal, in London
2013	Meena Upadhyaya establishes awards to celebrate ethnic minority women in Wales
2015	The creative production team including Annie Atkins wins an Academy Award for *The Grand Budapest Hotel*
2016	Jade Jones wins her second Olympic gold medal, in Rio
2019	Sali Mali celebrates 50 years in print and a Mary Quant exhibition is held at the V&A

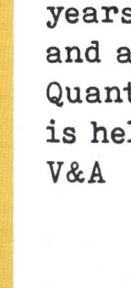

91

Phoebe Beatrix Bear ★ Angelica Zoë Bear ★ Annabelle Rose O'Neill ★ Olivia Rae Walker Robson
Evelyn Nansi Hughes ★ Libby Anne Stone ★ Rebecca Jayne McLay ★ Aoife Gwen Davies
Posey John ★ Bronwen Eira Mahoney ★ Elin Rhiannon Mahoney ★ Eirlys Moore
Ffion Moore ★ Nansi Eleri Beatrice Adams ★ Rania Aziz ★ Zahra Aziz ★ Willow Davies
Lois Haf Botwood ★ Amie Hoi-Ying Wong ★ Mali Gwen Dixon ★ Eleri Catryn Munn
Ruby Seren Caunter ★ Branwen Mari Crockett ★ Mali Haf Crockett ★ Poppy Willow Bryon
Mollie Fern Bryon ★ Casia Primrose Davies ★ Isra Zaman ★ Pearl Lila Taylor
Izzy Lawley ★ Eliza Lawley ★ Lleucu Brooker-Davies ★ Chloe Haf Heald ★ Elizabeth Catrin
Awel Clare ★ Nyah Martin ★ Stella Dyfi Hides ★ Aara Gwenllian Powel ★ Ruby Sian Lewis
Alys Sofia Ortu ★ Isabella Anna Ortu ★ Beti Blodyn Woodward ★ Rosalyn Aileen Isabel Bald
Ariana-May Phillips ★ Carenza Isabel Morgan ★ Alexandria Violet Morgan
Emily Elizabeth Marissen ★ Sophia Golubchikova ★ Sophia Grace Jones ★ Zara Rose Jones
Cariad Evans ★ Adelina Rae Loynton ★ Margot Emmeline Loynton ★ Seren Pitt
Sabrina Wei Tang-Rouse ★ Paisley Rose Roberts ★ Lizzie Houghton ★ Amy Houghton
Sophie Cannon-Jones ★ Alex Cannon-Jones ★ Gracie Anne Wilson ★ Sadie Greenley
Ffiôn Megan Ruth Price ★ Eiriol Llinos Ruth Price ★ Lydia Andrews ★ Millie Rose
Florence Elharhari ★ Alys Haf Bannister ★ Matilda Jane Magor ★ Emma-Lyn May Crisp
Heulwen Alua Thomas ★ Imogen Cate Griffiths ★ Gwen Stephens ★ Ava Morgan Lloyd
Coral Elsie Boucher ★ Cara Fox Shannon ★ Beatrice Teresa Neely
Mariyah Sarah Benmokaddem ★ Eleri Seren Keddle ★ Efa Iris Francis ★ Lilly Rose Howells
Jenna Mae Cobner ★ Mya Hardd James ★ Elena Quinn James. ★ Ivy Gwena Crouch-Puzey
Vada Georgina Ralph ★ Isabelle Edie Kinsella ★ Lacey Ela Lloyd ★ Georgia Grace Lewis
Betsy Eira Doyle ★ Maisie Rose Doyle ★ Isabella Reardon ★ Ella Violet Ann Barry
Annie Law ★ Ruby Haf James ★ Summer-Jane Mercer ★ Holly-Jane Mercer
Jestina Lillian Blackburn ★ Annabel Seren Kenney ★ Cadi Yorke Emmerson
Isabelle Benham ★ Ella-Rose Alford ★ Demie Seren ★ Macey Enfys ★ Salima Suleymanova
Safiya Suleymanova ★ Lottie Harden ★ Zara Harden ★ Espe Evelina Yuen-man Cambridge
Clara Rosemarie Insell ★ Lucy Beatrice Insell ★ Brogan Lilly Bassett ★ Esme Leanne Crocker
Hannah Irene Crocker ★ Emily Wallis ★ Sophie Wallis ★ Maddie Meller

Annie Olivia Dennis ★ Aoife Emily Brown ★ Lily Ann Owen ★ Sophie Ann Owen
Eleri Megan Ronan ★ Harriet Stephenson ★ Imogen Stephenson ★ Lily Hâf Davies
Emilia Catrin House ★ Amelia Mai Beaumont ★ Gwenno Haf Jones ★ Catrin Vanessa James
Phoebe Grace Mahoney ★ Betsan Mair Thomas ★ Catrin Haf Evans ★ Bella Elizabeth Wooller
Gwenllian-Fflur Antionette Williams ★ Elsabeth Hâf Lloyd ★ Grace Tottle
Lotti Eluned Mon Evans ★ Cerys Pearson ★ Summer Enfys Rose Shea ★ Sophia Pickford
Ava Pickford ★ Aria Pearl Murphy ★ Scarlett Isobel Murphy ★ Poppy Seren Edwards
Carys Elizabeth Jones ★ Meia Elin Evans ★ Elsa Aneurin Evans ★ Ana-Lucia Thomas
Isabelle Evelyn Humphreys ★ Megan Annabelle Owen ★ Cora May Roberts ★ Riva Phillips
Maddison Gloria Jane Jones ★ Celyn Louise Holloway ★ Rosaline Maloney
Niamh Maloney ★ Megan Fiona Mai Wright ★ Elwen Mary Elizabeth Wright ★ Maggie Hopkins
Scarlett Lily Evans ★ Bess Aneira Davies ★ Alys Ffion ★ Ellie Mair Tansley
Beth Tuxworth-Jones ★ Nia Evans ★ Celyn Matthews-Williams ★ Cara Alyse Smith
Aiya Neyazy ★ Roxy Jay Evans ★ Gwenan Haf Hughes ★ Mari Wen Hughes ★ Lucy Amelia Terry
Holly Nolan Terry ★ Layla Ashour ★ Orla Hâf Dowling ★ Rebecca Breeze ★ Anna Fflur James
Jessica Goldsworthy ★ Emma Goldsworthy ★ Emily Ophelia Tan ★ Cadi Awen Thomas
Swyn Fflur Thomas ★ Gwenllian Angharad Thomas ★ Carys Haf Hale ★ Amelie Esme Jones
Erin Morgan Chennells ★ Logan James Marin ★ Maia Airlie Chadwick ★ Millie Ann Chadwick
Mia Isabelle Watts ★ Bronwen Martha Roberts ★ Carys Mai Maxwell-Lyte ★ Anwen Mair Griffin
Kitty May Slater ★ Lola-Rose Kucia ★ Matilda Lily Lloyd-Hughes ★ Niah Grace Mumin
Ember Thomas-Welch ★ Millie Close ★ Rosie Bald ★ Matilda Felicia Prevel
Gabby Harding ★ Ruth Eleanor Anne Holt ★ Zoe Marie Cox ★ PennyLane Prudence Hambly
Megan Sara Richardson ★ Sadie Morgan Thomas ★ Jemima Kenny ★ Marnie Bella Bridgeman
Darcy Lewis ★ Lucee Marie Elisia Benyon ★ Millie Smith ★ Flora Smith
Brianny-Mai Trott ★ Elsie-Jaye Trott ★ Lowri Elizabeth Poynter ★ Alanna-Mai Evans
Isabella Louise Mills ★ Mollie Josephine Popham ★ Maggie Cora Stephens ★ Poppy Niamh Stephens
India Yeomans ★ Adelaide Watkins ★ Naomi Rees ★ Georgia McComas ★ Victoria Njie
Lucia Bridson ★ Jessica Finch ★ Talitha Appleby ★ Eleri Fenton-May ★ Evey Madeleine Gill
Zara Sandford-Taylor ★ Elinor Angela Stubbs ★ Amelia Bidhendy ★ Anna Roberts

Aoife Foley ★ Daisy Bolwell ★ Darcy Poyner ★ Ffion Skuse ★ Freya Reymond
Imogen Evans ★ Imogen Powell ★ Isabella Dewer ★ Ivy Lenahan ★ Jess Leyshon
Lowri Beckett ★ Nell Edmunds ★ Niamh Bowen ★ Olivia Knight ★ Rowen Longmuir
Seren Hayden ★ Violet Rogers ★ Zoe Goodwin ★ Mia Eluned Lewis
Alba Phillips ★ Clara Devine Viadiu ★ Gabrielle Heard ★ Isobel Evans ★ Sofia Evans
Lucy Charlotte Blake ★ Amy Violet Blake ★ Indigo Nova Bevan ★ Phoenix Scarlett Bevan
Isabella Eve Tinsley ★ Alice Evelyn Tinsley ★ Evelyn Hay ★ Alyssa Jessica Phillips
Lillie Iris Parfitt ★ Evie England ★ Alba Elsie Indiana Hamilton
Bonnie Blue Edmunds-Pavett ★ Betsie Beau Edmunds-Pavett ★ Scarlet Lily Rogers
Imogen Skylar Coffey ★ Tegan Amelia Lewis ★ Deryn Anne Page ★ Lilwen Ford
Lowri Isabella Vardon ★ Jenny Broadbent ★ Belle Gooch ★ Louisa Hillman ★ Zara Collins
Gwennan Elizabeth Savic ★ Ava Grace Sloan ★ Molly Louisa Sloan ★ Aurora Evans
Emilia Jones ★ Freja Ella Rees ★ Martha Rose Lane ★ Etta Faye Lane ★ Sarah Anahi Akmal
Imogen Annabell Betteridge ★ Felicity Gwendalynn Betteridge ★ Ffion Walter-Jones
Kitty Ada Jude Wilson ★ Phoebe Jay Rose Mages ★ Emelia Betty Blomquist ★ Jessica Lily Cooke
Maisie-Lee Lowri James ★ Evie Marie Jenkins ★ Molly Louise Jenkins
Liara Ophelia Gatica-Wilcox ★ Mair Caron Hopkins ★ Elin Ann Hopkins ★ Lilly Rose Morris
Mia Carys Jenkins ★ Bella Charley Evans ★ Lottie Mae Owens ★ Sophie Hopkins
Amélie Rose Bowen ★ Jasmine Megan Yeo ★ Isabella Seren Yeo ★ Cerys Tegan Jessica Gliddon
Ffion Elise Gliddon ★ Holly Rhiannon Gliddon ★ Rebecca Quelch ★ Mya Grace Oliver
Matilda Rose Stanley ★ Emily Ann Martin ★ Isabelle Mae Martin ★ Erin Mia Jones
Leila Non Jones ★ Mea Rebecca Sayce-Edwards ★ Georgina Louise Edwards ★ Sayami Rai
Harva Rose Evans ★ Maggie Elizabeth Sheehy ★ Ruby Celyn Howell ★ Zofia Carys Poręba
Milena Eleri Poręba ★ Cassandra Arianwen Maye Bruce-Lloyd ★ Lillie Alice Pritchard
Rosanna Sarah May Page ★ Anwen McCullough ★ Jessica Mary Anne Watson ★ Poppy Louise Davies
Cara Elena Morris-Roberts ★ Darcy Cotterill ★ Fleur Cotterill ★ Myemuna Barry
Maisie Harris ★ Enfys Mari Williams ★ Ela Martha Thomas ★ Megan Elizabeth Cowley
Amy Kathryn Hâf Eynon ★ Carys Mali-Rae Williams ★ Leusa Medi Llwyd ★ Emelia Seren Clay
Isla Louise Clay ★ Isabelle Jasmine Evans-Critten ★ Anest Mari Thomas ★ Madlen Eira Thomas

Daisy Abney-Hastings ★ Zelda Abney-Hastings ★ Carin Miriam ★ Jessica Smith-Jones
Charlotte Smith-Jones ★ Emily Smith-Jones ★ Annabelle Bray ★ Alaw Mair Jones
Eryn Mair Jenkins ★ Alaw Fflur Evans ★ Bonnie Louise Briwnant Jones
Mabli Gwenllian Booth ★ Thea Eira Lewis ★ Isla Celyn Lewis ★ Nia Poppy Wilkie
Isla Rose Rees ★ Ismay Eira White ★ Caitlin Rees Roberts ★ Elin Annwyl Winney
Amelia Lily Surgey ★ Ella Nicole Middleton ★ Sienna Rae Middleton
Phelicity Ocean Fenner ★ Phae Ellen Fenner ★ Phlo Ivy Fenner ★ Phoebe Mia Fenner
Malaika Teleri Dawson ★ Amelie Seren Dawson ★ Beca Mari Rees ★ Cari Elin Rees
Cari Calan Edwards ★ Etta Lyn Prytherch Woodland ★ Arwen Sara Edwards
Tirion Lois Edwards ★ Snow Lilly-Ann Sabat ★ Grace Ann Rose Roberts-Loosley
Soffia Elin Chaudhuri ★ Efa Celyn Buswell ★ Kiana Harlow Berner ★ Iyla Neveah Berner
Ela Mai Lewis ★ Rhoswen Myfanwy Margaret Evans ★ Poppy-Rae Griffiths ★ Polly Joseph
Hâf Louise Grasham ★ Rosa Dwynwen Davies ★ Scarlett Holland ★ Mia Gornall
Amaia Sofia Bella Charles ★ Seren Dorothy Bates ★ Evalyn Jean Martin
Ava Chloe Valentine-Harris ★ Elsi Sofia Davies ★ Anáis Honer ★ Olivia Honer ★ Shye Honer
Arabella Coulson ★ Ava Chloe Valentine ★ Bebe Louise Davies-Vice ★ Ruby Ann Ainslie Evans
Sofia Jean Eleanor Evans ★ Evie Ann Lindsay Evans ★ Esmae Rachel Joanne Stacey
Harriet Rose Hughes ★ Maisey Hughes ★ Georgie Hughes ★ Jersey Swann
Larna Riekstins - Morgan ★ Lily Hughes ★ Georgiana Hughes ★ Eva Bennett ★ Sian Jones
Scarlett Bowen ★ Erin Rogers ★ Alice Hughes ★ Riley Swann ★ Martha Lewis
Menna Thomas ★ Layla Williams ★ Eva Gardner ★ Erin Medi Roberts ★ Betsan Lili Whitehead
Millie Rose Pickup ★ Manon Fflur Davies ★ Liwsi Win Morgan Martin ★ Emillia Sherbon
Cadi Fflur Morgan Martin ★ Caitlin Pugh ★ Kate January-McCann ★ Clementine Gee
Rosemary Gee ★ Andrea MacDonald ★ Heidi Underwood ★ Fflur Arwel
Catherine Elan Taylor ★ Annette Smith ★ Gwenllian Jones

★ ★ WONDROUS WOMEN of WALES ★

Find the Dragon!

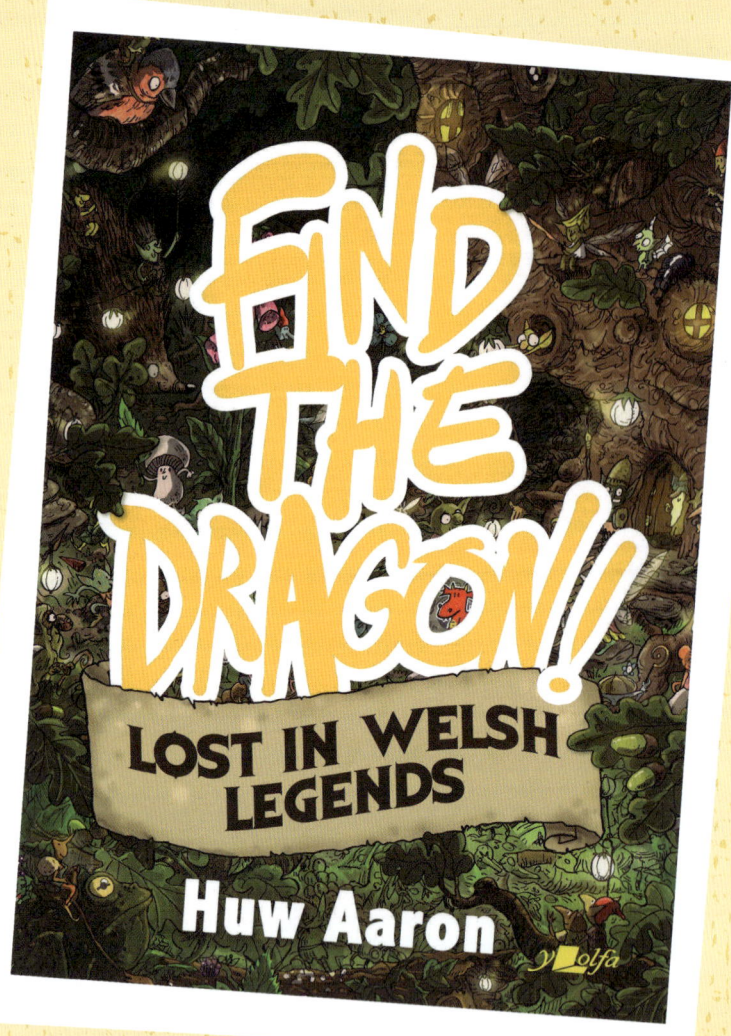

Find the Dragon! Lost in Welsh Legends

Huw Aaron

Two fun books packed with lively double-page illustrations – can you find the little red dragon hiding in each picture? Hours of fun for both children and adults, with a list of loads of other things to search for at the back of each book!